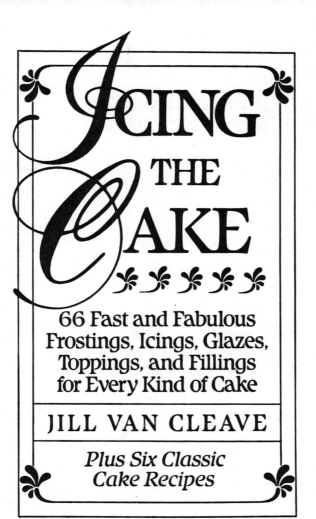

ICING THE CAKE

66 Fast and Fabulous
Frostings, Icings, Glazes,
Toppings, and Fillings
for Every Kind of Cake

JILL VAN CLEAVE

*Plus Six Classic
Cake Recipes*

CB
CONTEMPORARY
BOOKS
CHICAGO

Library of Congress Cataloging-in-Publication Data

Van Cleave, Jill.
    Icing the cake : 66 fast and fabulous frostings, icings, glazes,
toppings, and fillings for every kind of cake / Jill Van Cleave.
        p.   cm.
    Includes index.
    ISBN 0-8092-4115-3 : $7.95
    1. Icings, Cake.   I. Title.
TX771.V34   1990
641.8'653—dc20   90-35811
                                                    CIP

For my husband, Bill, whose constant enthusiasm
for his next meal serves as inspiration for our
shared life's work

Published by Contemporary Books, Inc.
180 North Michigan Avenue, Chicago, Illinois 60601
Manufactured in the United States of America
International Standard Book Number: 0-8092-4115-3

Contents

Acknowledgments

I want to give special thanks to the following people: Barry Bluestein, for making this book possible and my life easier; Linda Gray, for her vision, fine editorial direction, and faith; Georgene Sainati, for her creative, inspired art direction; Joseph W. Fell, for his expertise with the mechanics of computer set-up; Barbara Schaffner, for her patient instruction on the word processor; and Bill, for his skilled guidance and loving support.

Introduction

Dessert is the grand finale of any menu, and more often than not it is a cake that helps finish the festivities on a memorable note. Because presentation is as important as taste, this book is designed to help you top off the meal as well as the cake. Within these pages are dozens of elegant, easy-to-make recipes for frostings, fillings, sauces, and garnishes that will transform, in minutes, what might have been a rather ordinary cake into a special treat.

It is possible for you to create a dessert that pleases the eye and the palate without using special skills and fancy decorating equipment, or taking up hours and hours of valuable time. An ordinary chocolate cake can become extraordinary with the addition of a silken Cinnamon Cream Topping. Plain pound cake takes on a lively personality when spruced up with Ginger Icing. A store-bought sponge cake can become your own signature dessert when you fill it with Mocha Mousse or frost it with Praline Buttercream.

In Chapter 6 you will find six great cake recipes (including variations on these popular classics) that can be complemented with one of any number of toppings to suit the mood you wish to create. I urge you not only to try these cake recipes but also to use your own family favorites, or even a boxed cake mix or a plain store-bought cake. Whatever the base, here you have 66 different frostings, fillings, icings, glazes, toppings, sauces, and garnishes to choose from—allowing you to add your own special touch to every cake you serve.

1
Equipment

Pans of correct size, accurate measurements, and proper tools are must-haves for good baking. The equipment listed here is recommended for the recipes in this book.

Baking pans: For cake baking, you should have at least two 8-inch round cake pans, two 9-inch round cake pans, a regular 9″ × 5″ × 2½″ loaf pan, a standard fluted 12-cup bundt pan, a 9-inch springform pan (removable bottom), and a 15″ × 11″ jelly-roll pan with ¾″ sides. You can bake all of the cakes in this book with these pans, and they are standard sizes for many other baking recipes. Other useful pans are a 13″ × 9″ sheet pan and a flat cookie sheet. Avoid using thin aluminum pans. They are not sturdy and can buckle in the oven.

Measuring utensils: Use glass measuring cups for measuring liquid ingredients. Three sizes are useful: 1-cup, 2-cup, and 4-cup. Dry measuring cups come in nested sets and are made of stainless steel, plastic, or aluminum. Measuring spoons also come nested. For convenience you might want to own at least two sets of each.

Sifter: If you own one, use it. But a sifter is unnecessary if you have a fine-mesh sieve (which is also useful for straining). Place dry ingredients in a sieve over a mixing bowl and stir with a spoon to sift them.

Mixing bowls: Two sets are handy: one stainless-steel nested set and one glass nested set.

Electric mixer: A portable hand-held mixer is fine for whipping cream and eggs or mixing soft batters and frostings. A stationary, heavy-duty countertop mixer, however, is more versatile. Only two countertop mixer attachments are necessary for the recipes in this book: a flat paddle (for cake batters and general creaming, blending, and mixing) and a wire whip (for beating, whipping, and blending ingredients such as liquids, eggs, cream, and melted chocolate). Buy two stainless-steel mixing bowls to use when you are preparing recipes that call for mixing two separate preparations.

Electric blender: The blender has a myriad of uses. You will need it to puree fruit for recipes in this book.

Timer: Set your timer for the shortest suggested baking time. You can always reset it for more time if the cake doesn't test done.

Oven thermometer: Heat your oven or ovens and test for accurate temperature readings from time to time, as an incorrectly calibrated oven can ruin a cake. The small aluminum thermometers sold in supermarkets are not the most reliable. Look for a mercury thermometer in a fold-up stainless-steel case, sold in cookware stores.

Wire racks: These are useful for cooling cakes and other baked items. Those that are round or square, made of sturdy stainless steel, are best. Buy several.

Cake tester: This is a convenience, not a necessity. To test baked cakes for doneness, a long, thin piece of wire can substitute, as can a toothpick or long needle.

Cardboard rounds/cake plates: Cardboard rounds are very useful for catching drips and smears when you are frosting a cake. You will find them in various sizes in cookware stores. Use a size slightly larger than your cake, and then transfer the finished cake to a clean platter. Cake plates are flat with no rim and come with or without a pedestal. A turntable on a pedestal can be a valuable asset when you frost and garnish cakes.

Saucepans: Look for heavy-gauge, steel-bottomed pans, which are perfect for cooking sugar or sugar syrups. Lighter-weight pans are likely to develop hot spots that may cause sugar to burn. Porcelain-coated cast-iron pans are useful for making egg and custard sauces.

Double boiler: Use a stainless steel double boiler or a porcelain pan nested in a bottom pan of copper. A double boiler is not an essential piece of equipment if you own stainless-steel saucepans and a set of stainless-steel mixing bowls. Just be sure to select a bowl that fits snugly onto the saucepan rim, and always leave space between the bottom of the bowl and the water in the pan below.

Whisks: It will be useful to have at least a couple of sizes on hand to smoothly blend various quantities of ingredients, whip cream, and beat eggs. A whisk is also used to fold beaten egg whites or whipped cream into another ingredient.

Rubber spatulas: These are inexpensive, and you can never have too many. Be sure to buy heat-resistant spatulas. Use them for stirring, combining, folding, and transferring mixtures.

Icing and metal spatulas: An icing spatula usually has a wooden handle and a thin (1-inch to 1½-inch), flexible metal blade. They're used for spreading frostings, icing, glazes, and toppings. Cake spatulas, tapered in the triangular shape of a layer cake slice, will aid in serving. Wide pancake-type spatulas (two) are useful in transferring a frosted cake to a serving platter or cake plate.

Grater/shredder: The standard hand-held, four-sided stainless-steel grater has both coarse-shred and fine-grate options. Use fine grate to remove the rind from citrus fruit.

Peelers: A citrus peeler is a great tool for removing the peel of citrus in long, thin spirals. A vegetable peeler can be used for peeling citrus skin as well.

Miscellaneous: Mixing spoons (wooden and other), pastry brushes or paint brushes, a rolling pin, a ruler, and a citrus juicer are all helpful, as are good-quality knives. A chef's knife, a serrated knife, a slicing knife, and a paring knife are the bare minimum to have on hand.

2
Ingredients

In selecting ingredients, be concerned about freshness, flavor, and quality, and you will be ahead of the game before you begin to cook. What follows is a list of common baking ingredients, with details on how and why each is used in a recipe.

Baking powder: This provides leavening to expand cake batters. The most commonly available variety is double-acting baking powder. Even stored in a cool, dry place, baking powder will lose its strength after about one year.

Baking soda: This is used as a substitute for baking powder in recipes that call for sour dairy products or acid ingredients such as citrus. The soda reacts with the acid to provide leavening during baking, much the way baking powder does. It has a long shelf life but lumps when exposed to humidity, making it difficult to measure. Sifting before measuring may be necessary.

Butter: Unsalted butter is used in many dessert recipes, including those in this book. Made from sweet cream with no added salt, it has a delicate, fresh flavor. The lack of salt, however, also means it is more perishable than salted butter. Keep refrigerated no longer than two weeks. Freeze for longer storage.

Cake flour: This is finely milled, soft-wheat flour with less protein (gluten) than all-purpose flour. It gives baked cakes a soft, crumbly texture. All-purpose flour, on the other hand, produces dense and heavier cakes. If you must, you can substitute ⅞ cup of all-purpose flour for 1 cup of cake flour.

Cocoa powder: Use only unsweetened cocoa powder for baking. Dutch-processed cocoa powder is alkalinized and gives a slightly richer chocolate flavor than the nonalkalinized type. There are several brands on the market. Use the one you prefer.

Cornstarch and arrowroot: Cornstarch, a starchy flour made from corn, is used for thickening liquids, particularly sauces. Arrowroot, a less common starch also used for thickening, gives a more translucent quality to thickened sauces than cornstarch. Arrowroot thickens liquid just before the boiling point, whereas liquid with cornstarch must be boiled at least 30 seconds before it thickens properly. Dissolve either starch in cool water or another liquid before adding to hot or simmering liquid to avoid lumping. Either starch may be added directly to ingredients before they are heated. Stir constantly until thickened for smooth blending.

Crème fraîche: This French cousin of sour cream has a lively, slightly sour flavor with a consistency closer to whipped cream than sour cream. It can be purchased in the dairy section of specialty food markets or made at home from whipping cream and buttermilk. Various cookbooks offer recipes for these home-prepared versions. For those not able to obtain crème fraîche, I've included an alternative ingredient you can use in each of the recipes calling for it.

Eggs: Grade A large eggs are the standard size in most recipes for baked foods. Use eggs at room temperature to achieve the best volume and texture. A quick method to remove the chill of cold eggs is to immerse them in a bowl of warm water for 10 minutes before using them. Separate eggs carefully to avoid breaking the yolk. (You may want to do this over an extra bowl so that mistakes can be caught.) When using already separated eggs, measure 1 tablespoon yolk and 2 tablespoons white for the equivalent of 1 large egg.

Gelatin: Gelatin is used to congeal liquids into a semisolid state. A small amount causes softly whipped cream to stabilize (remain firm), while a larger amount will solidify it. Use envelopes of unflavored gelatin for jelling purposes. One envelope of gelatin will jell 2 cups of liquid. When working with gelatin, sprinkle the granules over a liquid and let them soak a minute to set. Warm the mixture to melt and dissolve the gelatin, but do not let it boil. Use it in recipes while it is still liquid, before it has cooled and set. When adding liquefied gelatin to cold ingredients, beat constantly to avoid lumping, as the gelatin will begin to set rapidly.

Sugars: Granulated sugar may be generally considered all-purpose, but it is too coarse for use in uncooked frostings and toppings. Superfine sugar is very fine and is an ingredient in buttercream frostings and other recipes in which the sugar has to dissolve quickly. Confectioners' sugar has been refined to a powder. It contains a small amount of cornstarch to prevent lumping. Confectioners' sugar dissolves instantly in liquid and has a smoothness desirable in frostings, icings, and whipped cream toppings. Brown sugar, light and dark, has the flavor of molasses in varying degrees. Its moisture content causes this sugar to harden when it is not wrapped in an airtight bag or container. Pack light and dark brown sugar into measuring cups and spoons before using.

Vanilla extract: Use pure vanilla extract. There are several good varieties on the market. For optimum flavor, add vanilla (and any other extract) to a cooked mixture *after* it has been removed from heat. Imitation vanilla should be avoided—it's a woefully poor substitute for real vanilla flavor.

Whipping cream: This is heavy cream, which contains between 32 and 40 percent butterfat. Whipping cream is best whipped cold in a chilled bowl, either at medium speed with a wire whip attachment or by hand with a wire whisk. During whipping, the cream will pass through three stages. First it thickens, then it forms soft peaks and finally it forms stiff peaks. Overwhipped cream turns to butter. The best way for a novice to learn to recognize the three stages of whipped cream is to sacrifice a cup for the learning experience and make it into butter.

3
How to Melt Chocolate

Whether semisweet, bittersweet, or unsweetened, chocolate must be handled with care when it is melting. Excessive heat and water are the enemies of smoothly melting chocolate. Cocoa butter and other solid vegetable shortenings are the allies. Usually, when melting chocolate suddenly seizes up (tightens and breaks), the cause is either too much heat (chocolate heated to too high a temperature or heated for too long a time) or the accidental addition of as little as one drop of liquid. If heat (above 120°F) has scorched the chocolate, it is lost. You must begin again with new chocolate. If liquid has caused the problem, you can correct it by stirring a tablespoon (or more, if necessary) of solid vegetable shortening into the chocolate.

Use any of the following procedures for melting chocolate.

Microwave oven: Once you try this method, it surely will become the preferred one. Chop the chocolate into small pieces, for even melting, and place them in a glass bowl. Set uncovered in the microwave oven. Microwave on high power until the chocolate is almost melted but still slightly lumpy (between 1 and 2 minutes). Once chocolate is out of the oven, a little stirring will usually finish the melting. If it needs more heat, put it back into the microwave oven for an additional 30 seconds.

Double boiler: Bring the water in the bottom pan just barely to simmer. Bubbles should not form. The surface should be barely moving. Place chopped chocolate in the top of the double boiler or in a stainless-steel mixing bowl that fits snugly into the pan without touching the water. Stir, uncovered, until the mixture is just melted. Remove from heat carefully. Steam droplets sometimes find their way into the chocolate with this method, which is why the heat must be kept low.

Oven: Professional chefs often use this method because it is convenient. Heat the oven to 250° F. Place chopped chocolate, in a stainless-steel bowl, in the oven and heat the chocolate until it is almost melted, but still slightly lumpy (10 to 15 minutes). Take the chocolate out of the oven and stir it to finish the melting.

Adding Ingredients

When you add ingredients to melted chocolate, don't be shy! It's a *small* amount of liquid that causes chocolate to seize. Fatty substances such as butter and cream can be added to chocolate before it is melted as long as you add more than just a small amount. Heated cream or milk can be poured over chopped chocolate and stirred until the chocolate melts. Sometimes a recipe calls for adding a flavoring to melted chocolate. Any liquid flavoring added should be at room temperature or slightly warm, never chilled.

4
Some Terms Defined

These terms, referred to again and again in dessert recipes, may confuse the inexperienced baker.

Cream: Beat ingredients until smoothly blended. Butter is usually creamed until softened, or creamed with sugar. Cream cheese can be creamed like butter. Cream the ingredients, which should be at room temperature, with the flat beater in an electric mixer or by hand. Cold butter or cream cheese can be softened in the microwave oven on high power for 20 to 30 seconds without melting.

Stir: Stirring is best done by hand with a spoon or rubber spatula. It is not a vigorous motion and is done in circular strokes.

Beat: Beating must be vigorous. It is also best done with an electric mixer, although a strong arm and wooden spoon can accomplish the same thing. A whisk, or wire whip, is used to beat items that need blending as well as beating.

Whip: Whipping is beating with a wire whip or whisk to incorporate air into an ingredient or mixture. Cream should be whipped cold, egg whites at room temperature. Both must be whipped in clean bowls with clean beaters. "Softly beaten" means the mixture is still soft enough to fold back onto itself. "Stiffly beaten" means the mixture is stiff enough to retain a shape.

Fold: Folding is done by hand only, using a rubber spatula or whisk. The objective is the gentle blending of whipped or beaten ingredients into a combined whole without losing volume. With an even sweeping stroke, cut down through the center of the mixture to the bowl bottom, then pull up and over the top. Repeat this action while giving your bowl quarter turns. Fold only until ingredients are just blended together. Be careful not to overblend, because the mixture will begin deflating with excessive folding.

5
Start-to-Finish Techniques and Tips for Cake Baking

Baking and decorating a cake that you present proudly, knowing it is attractive, flavorful, and satisfying from the first look to the last bite, is a worthy accomplishment. Furthermore, preparing such a cake need not be a frustrating, difficult, or overly time-consuming process. Naturally, the more you bake the easier it becomes. But even for those attempting their first from-scratch cake, the experience can be painless and gratifying.

The route to successful baking is paved with some basic techniques and tips you should know. These are simple steps that can be applied to most cake recipes.

Substitutions

Try to use the ingredients specified. If you substitute margarine for butter, the cake will still be a good one, but it won't be rich and buttery tasting. If you substitute jumbo eggs for large eggs, however, you will upset the balance of liquid-to-dry ingredients, and the resulting cake will be different from the one the recipe is designed to produce. Cakes baked with cake flour are crumblier than those baked with all-purpose flour. It is best not to substitute ingredients until you are an experienced baker.

Measurement

Every cake is a precise, if uncomplicated, scientific formula. In baking, nothing is more important than measuring accurately, so use the appropriate measuring tools: glass measuring cups for liquid ingredients, correct-sized measuring cups for dry ingredients, and measuring spoons. Liquid measuring cups should sit on a flat surface, with liquid poured in and measured at eye level for accuracy. Dry cup measures should be "scooped and scraped." Dip the measuring cup directly into the dry ingredient (such as flour) and scoop it up. The cup will be overfilled. Scrape the top from one side to the other with the flat side of a table knife to even it off. You should also use the knife to scrape the tops of measuring spoons.

Temperature

In cake baking it is preferable to have ingredients at room temperature. This will facilitate smooth creaming, better volume, and make cakes more tender. Check the temperature of your heated oven with an oven thermometer, and, if necessary, adjust the thermostat knob to correct the temperature. Baking a cake at an incorrect temperature is bound to give unsatisfactory results.

Greasing the Pans

Cake pans should be evenly greased with butter or other solid shortening unless otherwise noted in the recipe. Apply softened fat with a paper towel or pastry brush.

Assembly

Read through each recipe completely before you begin. Measure (and sift, if necessary) and assemble the needed ingredients, equipment, and tools at your work space. If two or more ingredients require creaming, mix until smoothly blended and lightened in color before adding another ingredient. Eggs provide the cake's volume, so add eggs one at a time, beating after each addition. The dry ingredients should be blended into the batter thoroughly but not too much, because overbeating can toughen a cake. It is best to reduce mixer speed to medium (or lower) when adding the dry ingredients, and then mix no longer than 2 minutes.

Baking

Batter poured into a pan should be evenly dispersed before baking. Shake, tilt, and tap pans on a countertop to smooth out the batter. (An exception is sponge cake batter, which should *not* be tapped down in pans, as this action could deflate the volume. In this case, smooth the batter with a rubber spatula.) Bake cakes in the middle of the oven. Do not let pans touch the oven walls. To determine whether a cake has been fully baked, insert a cake tester or toothpick into the center of the cake, remove it, and check to see whether any uncooked batter clings to the tester or pick. When the cake is fully baked, the tester or pick will come out clean. Other signs that the cake is done are a set center, a springy top that pulls slightly away from the sides of the pan, and smell. A delicious aroma wafting through the kitchen is a signal to test your cake for doneness.

Cooling

Set a just-baked cake on a wire rack. This allows air to circulate under the cake pan to cool it. Invert the cake while it's still warm and remove it from the pan to cool completely on the rack. A cake should be cooled to room temperature before it is cut or frosted. An exception is when a flavored syrup or glaze is to be absorbed into the cake. In this case, the cake is brushed while it is still warm.

Storing

What do you do when time does not allow for baking and frosting in the same day? Bake and cool the cake or cake layers as directed in the recipe. Then wrap the cake in plastic wrap or aluminum foil (wrap layers individually), set it aside at room temperature overnight, and frost it the following day. If you plan to bake ahead two days or more before doing the frosting, double-wrap and freeze the cake. Defrost the cake, in its wrapper, to room temperature before proceeding.

6
Cake Recipes

While these recipes have been designed with the novice baker in mind, more experienced cooks won't want to overlook them, either. Each recipe is straightforward and easy to prepare, and the resulting treat will satisfy anyone with a craving for the moist, delectable taste of a homemade cake.

Basic Butter Cake—White or Yellow

Yield: 2 8-inch layers

The child in all of us remembers this cake. It is what most of us ate at birthday parties and is probably the first cake we baked with a mother's or grandmother's guidance. As adults, this is the cake that comforts and pleases us most. Frost it with whatever suits your mood. A white or yellow butter cake is essentially the same cake, except that egg whites are used in the white cake, egg yolks in the yellow cake.

1 tablespoon unsalted butter	*1 cup granulated sugar*
2 cups cake flour	*4 large egg whites for white cake or 4*
2 teaspoons baking powder	*large egg yolks for yellow cake*
¼ teaspoon salt	*⅔ cup whole milk*
⅔ cup (1¼ sticks) unsalted butter	*1 teaspoon vanilla extract*

1. Heat oven to 350°F. Grease bottom and sides of two 8-inch round cake pans with 1 tablespoon of butter. Set pans aside.

2. Sift flour, baking powder, and salt together in a bowl. Set aside.

3. Cream ⅔ cup butter with sugar in a mixer on medium speed until smoothly blended and lightened in color. Beat in the egg whites or egg yolks. Increase mixer speed to medium high for 2 minutes.

4. Reduce mixer speed to medium low and add the sifted ingredients alternately with the milk. Add the vanilla and mix 1 minute longer.

5. Divide batter equally between the two cake pans. Shake pans, and then tap on table to evenly distribute batter. (Batter will barely fill pans halfway.) Bake in middle of the oven until inserted cake tester or toothpick comes out clean, about 25 minutes.

6. Set pans on wire racks. When pans have cooled to warm, invert them on cake plates or cardboard rounds to remove cakes. Let cakes cool completely before frosting.

Note: Wrap unfrosted cake layers individually in plastic wrap and leave at room temperature not longer than 2 days before using. Double-wrap if layers are to be frozen for later use.

Chocolate Layer Cake

Yield: 2 9-inch layers

Dark, fudgy, and moist, this cake is very easy to prepare.

1 tablespoon unsalted butter	½ teaspoon salt
1 tablespoon unsweetened cocoa powder	2 cups granulated sugar
½ cup (1 stick) unsalted butter	1½ cups buttermilk (see note)
1¾ cups cake flour	½ cup strong coffee
1 cup unsweetened cocoa powder	2 large eggs
2 teaspoons baking soda	2 teaspoons vanilla extract

1. Heat oven to 350°F. Grease bottom and sides of two 9-inch round cake pans with 1 tablespoon butter. Add 1 tablespoon cocoa powder to one cake pan. Tilt and roll the pan to evenly distribute cocoa; shake out excess into the second pan. Repeat to coat bottom and sides of second pan with cocoa. Shake out any excess. Set pans aside.

2. Melt ½ cup butter in a glass measuring cup in a microwave oven on high power for 1 minute. Or melt over low heat in a small saucepan and set aside.

3. Sift flour, 1 cup cocoa, soda, and salt into the bowl of an electric mixer Add sugar. Turn mixer onto low speed for 30 seconds to combine ingredients.

4. Increase speed to medium low. Add buttermilk, coffee, melted butter, eggs, and vanilla. Increase speed to medium and beat about 2 minutes.

5. Divide batter equally between the two cake pans, filling each about two-thirds full. Bake in middle of the oven until inserted cake tester or toothpick comes out clean, and cake is springy when touched, 35 to 40 minutes.

6. Set pans on wire racks. When pans have cooled to warm, invert them on cake plates or cardboard rounds. Cool completely before frosting.

Note: Wrap unfrosted cake layers individually in plastic wrap and leave at room temperature not longer than 2 days before using. Double-wrap if layers are to be frozen for later use

---

Note: Buttermilk substitution (for this recipe only): mix 1 cup whole milk with ½ cup sour cream.

(Not Quite So) Plain Pound Cake

Yield: 1 loaf

This is truly an effortless cake to make. It's perfect for many occasions and equally pleasing for breakfast or snacking. Instead of frosting the pound cake, try icing or glazing its domed top.

> ½ tablespoon unsalted butter
> 2 cups cake flour
> ½ teaspoon salt
> 1 teaspoon baking soda
> 1 cup (2 sticks) unsalted butter
> 1 cup granulated sugar
> 4 large eggs
> ⅔ cup sour cream
> 1½ teaspoons vanilla extract

1. Heat oven to 350°F. Grease a 9″ × 5″ × 2½″ loaf pan with ½ tablespoon butter.

2. Sift flour, salt, and soda into a bowl and set aside.

3. Cream 1 cup butter with sugar, using a mixer on medium speed, until mixture is smooth. Add the eggs one by one, blending mixture after each addition.

4. Add sour cream and blend. Reduce mixer speed to medium low and add sifted ingredients and vanilla. Blend 1 minute longer until batter is very smooth.

5. Pour batter into the loaf pan. Bake in middle of the oven until an inserted cake tester or toothpick comes out clean, 50 to 55 minutes. Set pan on wire rack to cool.

6. When pan has cooled to warm, invert it on the rack to remove cake. Let cake cool completely.

7. Glaze, if desired. Wait at least 1 hour before serving.

Note: You may wrap an unglazed cake in plastic wrap or aluminum foil and leave at room temperature for up to 3 days. Double-wrapped, it also freezes beautifully.

Pound Cake Flavor Variations

Lemon Pound Cake: Omit vanilla extract in ingredients list. Add grated rind of two lemons (2 to 3 teaspoons) and 2 tablespoons fresh lemon juice. Follow preparation instructions, adding the lemon rind and juice after the sifted ingredients in Step 4.

Praline Pound Cake: Prepare Praline (see Index) at least 1 day ahead. Reduce granulated sugar to ⅔ cup instead of 1 cup. Add ⅔ cup Praline after the sifted ingredients in Step 4. Reserve the remaining Praline for future garnish.

Applesauce Bundt Cake

Yield: 1 bundt cake

Fruit puree is the moistening ingredient for this tender cake. Purchase natural unsweetened applesauce, as applesauce made with sugar would oversweeten the cake. If making the banana variation, use ripe fruit (completely yellow and softened) for a pronounced flavor.

1 tablespoon unsalted butter
4 cups cake flour
1 teaspoon baking soda
½ teaspoon salt
2 teaspoons ground cinnamon
1 teaspoon ground nutmeg
2 cups (16 ounces) unsweetened applesauce
4 large eggs
2 teaspoons vanilla extract
1¼ cups (2½ sticks) unsalted butter
2 cups packed light brown sugar
1½ cups (6 ounces) chopped pecans

1. Heat oven to 350°F. Grease a 12-cup bundt pan with 1 tablespoon butter or substitute vegetable cooking spray. Nonstick-coated bundt pans need not be greased.

2. Combine flour, soda, salt, cinnamon, and nutmeg in a bowl. Stir to combine and set aside.

3. Stir applesauce, eggs, and vanilla together in another bowl. Set aside.

4. Cream 1¼ cups butter with sugar in a mixer on medium speed until smoothly blended and lightened in color.

5. Reduce mixer speed to low and add the dry ingredients alternately with the applesauce mixture. When blended, stir in nuts.

6. Pour batter into the bundt pan. Shake pan to evenly distribute batter. Bake in middle of the oven until top is browned and springy when touched, 50 to 60 minutes. Set pan on wire rack to cool.

7. When pan has cooled to warm, invert on rack to remove cake. Let cake cool completely.

8. Ice or glaze as desired. Place cake on cake plate at least an hour before serving. If serving is delayed, cover an iced cake with a bowl large enough to clear icing.

Note: You may wrap an uniced cake in aluminum foil and leave at room temperature for up to 2 days. Double-wrap before freezing.

FRUIT FLAVOR VARIATION

Banana Bundt Cake: Substitute 2 cups banana puree for the applesauce. Add ½ teaspoon lemon juice to banana puree to retard discoloration. Substitute walnuts for the pecans, if desired. Follow preparation instructions.

Classic Sponge Cake

Yield: 2 9-inch layers

Sponge cakes are airy and light, so they cool quickly after baking, a great advantage for hurried bakers. Any buttercream, mousse, or cream-based filling or frosting is a delicious addition to this type of cake.

TWO-LAYER SPONGE CAKE

1½ tablespoons butter or margarine	1 teaspoon vanilla extract
2 tablespoons granulated sugar	⅔ cup granulated sugar
6 large eggs	1 cup cake flour

1. Heat oven to 350°F. Generously grease bottom and sides of two 9-inch round cake pans with 1½ tablespoons butter or margarine. Add 2 tablespoons granulated sugar to one cake pan. Tilt and roll the pan to evenly distribute sugar on its bottom and sides; shake out excess into the second pan and repeat the coating process. Shake out any excess sugar and set pans aside.

2. Separate eggs; yolks go into one mixing bowl and whites into another. Sift cake flour into a third bowl.

3. Beat egg yolks with a mixer on high speed for 5 minutes. The yolks will lighten in color, thicken, and increase in volume. Stir vanilla into yolks and set aside.

4. Clean wire whip thoroughly and then immediately begin beating egg whites on medium speed until thickened and softly whipped. Sprinkle on ⅓ cup of the sugar and continue to beat until whites are stiff and glossy. (This should take about 5 minutes.)

5. Using a rubber spatula, fold the remaining ⅓ cup sugar into the beaten whites. Fold in the yolk mixture, and then fold in the sifted flour.

6. Divide batter evenly between the two cake pans. Smooth tops with the spatula. Bake in middle of the oven until tops are lightly golden and springy when touched, 20 to 25 minutes. Set pans on wire racks for 10 minutes.

7. Spread a clean dish towel on a countertop and invert pans on towel to unmold cakes. Let cakes cool completely before frosting.

Note: You may wrap unfrosted cake layers individually in plastic wrap and leave at room temperature not longer than 1 day before using. Double-wrap if layers are to be frozen for later use.

SPONGE CAKE FLAVOR VARIATION

Chocolate Sponge Cake: Reduce cake flour to ½ cup instead of 1 cup. Add ½ cup unsweetened cocoa powder. Sift cake flour with cocoa powder in Step 2 and follow preparation instructions.

SPONGE CAKE ROLL

Yield: 1 15″ × 11″ sheet cake

See the Classic Sponge Cake recipe on the facing page for ingredients and preparation instructions. Make roll from either the classic recipe or the chocolate variation, with the following changes:

1. Heat oven to 350°F. Generously grease bottom and sides of a 15″ × 11″ jelly-roll pan with 1½ tablespoons butter or margarine. Add 2 tablespoons granulated sugar to pan. Shake and tilt back and forth to distribute sugar evenly on pan bottom. Shake out any excess. Set pan aside.

Follow Steps 2 through 5 of the Classic Sponge Cake recipe. (For a chocolate sponge cake roll, refer to the directions at the end of the classic recipe.)

6. Pour batter into pan. Spread evenly with the spatula. Bake in middle of the oven until lightly golden and springy when touched, about 15 minutes. Set pan on wire rack for 5 minutes.

7. Spread a clean dish towel flat onto a countertop or work surface. Invert jelly-roll pan on towel and release cake from pan. While cake is still warm, roll it up in the towel. The towel will prevent the cake from sticking together while it cools in the rolled shape. Let cake cool completely.

8. When cake is cool, unroll and spread it with desired frosting or filling in an even layer, leaving a ¼-inch clear border around edges. Reroll cake and set it on a serving tray seam-side down. Trim a thin slice from each end. Frost or decorate outside of roll as desired.

Note: A filled sponge cake roll should be wrapped and refrigerated if it is not to be served within 4 hours.

Cheesecake

Yield: 1 9-inch cake

If a cake popularity contest were held, cheesecake would undoubtedly be the clear winner. A simple topping or glaze can add an elegant touch. This cookie crust, made from prepared cookie dough, is prebaked, and its delicious crunch complements the creamy filling.

10 ounces (½ 20-ounce package) prepared
*   refrigerated sugar cookie dough*
2 pounds (4 8-ounce packages) cream cheese,
*   at room temperature*
1½ cups granulated sugar
5 large eggs
2 tablespoons all-purpose flour
1 teaspoon grated lemon rind (1 lemon)
2 teaspoons vanilla extract
⅓ cup whipping cream

1. Heat oven to 350°F. Release bottom from a 9-inch springform pan.

2. Roll out cookie dough between two sheets of waxed paper into a 10-inch circle. Peel off top sheet. Place pan bottom, upside down, on center of dough. Lift from underneath the bottom sheet of waxed paper and turn over so dough is on top. Peel off the remaining sheet of paper. Trim excess dough from around pan edges and discard. Fit the dough-lined pan bottom back into the springform and close the spring. Bake until lightly golden, about 12 minutes. Set pan on wire rack to cool.

3. Lower oven heat to 325°F. (To prevent the baking cheesecake from cracking, add a bit of moisture to your oven by placing a shallow pan of water on a very low shelf in the oven.) Beat cream cheese in mixer on medium speed until soft. Add sugar and beat until smoothly blended. Add eggs, blending with each addition. Reduce mixer speed to medium low and add flour, lemon rind, vanilla, and cream.

4. Pour batter onto prepared crust. Set pan on a sheet pan and bake in middle of the oven until center is barely set and top is lightly golden and raised slightly, 1 hour to 1 hour and 10 minutes.

5. Set cake on wire rack to cool. Cover and refrigerate cooled cake in the pan for at least 4 hours before serving. Remove springform and cut cake into wedges. All cheesecakes should be cut with a knife that has been dipped into warm water.

Note: You may keep cheesecake stored in refrigerator, covered with plastic wrap, for up to 1 week. Topping or glaze should not be applied until within 4 hours of serving time. To freeze: carefully transfer chilled cake to a cardboard round and double-wrap with plastic wrap.

CHEESECAKE FLAVOR VARIATIONS

Strawberry Cheesecake: Omit vanilla extract and whipping cream in ingredients list. Puree 1 package (10 to 12 ounces) frozen unsweetened strawberries, thawed, in an electric blender. Measure out 1 cup strawberry puree. After grating lemon rind, squeeze 1 tablespoon juice from the lemon. Follow preparation instructions, adding the lemon juice and strawberry puree after lemon rind in Step 3. Garnish cake top with Easy Glazed Strawberries (see Index).

Mocha Cheesecake: Substitute 10 ounces ($\frac{1}{2}$ 20-ounce package) prepared refrigerated chocolate cookie dough for the sugar cookie dough. Omit grated lemon rind, vanilla extract, and whipping cream. Mix 2 tablespoons instant coffee granules with $\frac{1}{3}$ cup coffee liqueur and stir to dissolve the coffee. Follow preparation instructions, adding the coffee mixture after the flour in Step 3. Garnish cake top with Chocolate Glaze (see Index) or chocolate curls (see Index, "Chocolate Shapes and Curls").

7
Frostings

For some people, cake is just an excuse to eat frosting. For true frosting lovers it can rarely be too sweet, too creamy, or too rich.

The frosting recipes in this chapter provide something for everyone. Whether your preference is for sweet, buttery, creamy, rich-with-chocolate-or-fruit, or leaning-toward-bitter frosting, you'll find it here.

These frostings are of spreadable consistency, suitable for use as fillings between layers and for finishing off the sides and top of your cake. Each recipe indicates whether the frosting should be chilled before it is used or immediately spread onto a cake. Frosting consistencies vary, depending on ingredients, so follow the specific instructions. It will help, however, to have some basic information about frosting cakes before you begin.

The Basics

In preparation for frosting, place the cooled cake on a flat cake plate, cardboard round, or turntable that is at least 1 inch larger in diameter than the cake.

In the unlikely event that you should need to even off an unevenly baked cake before frosting it, simply cut horizontally across the cake with a slicing knife to remove the domed piece, making sure you are at eye level with the cake top.

Brush off any crumbs from the area you will be frosting. If the surface you are brushing continues to crumb, try these solutions before proceeding with the frosting: chill the cake layers, or brush the layers lightly with fruit glaze or melted jelly and let dry, or brush the layers with beaten egg white and let dry.

When creating a layer cake, spread the bottom layer evenly with frosting or filling, without being excessive. Position the top layer and press it down lightly onto the first.

To finish most cakes, use a thin metal spatula and frost the sides of the cake first with smooth back and forth strokes. What counts is covering the cake evenly, not thickness. Spread frosting onto the top last, using smooth gliding strokes across the cake. (For the smoothest result, sparsely frost your cake, chill it, and then add the remaining frosting.)

Transfer your frosted cake to a serving platter with the aid of one or two wide spatulas. (An extra cardboard round can be a useful substitute for a spatula.)

Set the frosted cake aside for 30 minutes or up to 4 hours before serving. Generally speaking, heat and frosted cakes don't mix. The temperature of a cool room (about 65°F) is ideal for short-term storage of most frosted cakes. If stored longer (more than 4 hours), cakes probably will require refrigeration. Specific storing instructions are appended to each frosting recipe. The easiest way to protect a cake without smearing the frosting or delicate decoration is to cover the cake with a bowl that does not touch the cake's top or sides.

This symbol, *, used in front of the name of a cake, means that the cake recipe can be found in this book.

Note: Frosting quantities—for an 8-inch, two-layer cake, you will need at least 2½ cups of frosting; for a 9-inch, two-layer cake, you will need at least 3 cups of frosting.

Cream Cheese Frosting with Orange Peel

~~~~~~~

Yield: 3 cups

The orange peel adds just a hint of flavor plus decorative flecks of color and texture to this classic cream cheese frosting.

12 ounces (1½ 8-ounce packages) cream cheese, at room
*   temperature*
⅓ cup (5⅓ tablespoons) unsalted butter, at room temperature
1½ teaspoons dried orange peel
2¼ cups confectioners' sugar

1. Beat cream cheese and butter together in a mixer on medium speed until softened. Add orange peel.

2. Add sugar, ½ cup at a time, until smoothly blended. Scrape down sides of bowl with rubber spatula as necessary.

3. Use immediately to frost cake, or cover and refrigerate until ready to use.

CAKES SUGGESTED FOR THIS FROSTING

*Basic Butter Cake (White or Yellow)
Carrot Cake
Spice Cake
Pecan or Walnut Cake

Coconut Cream Frosting

Yield: 3½ cups

The cream of coconut in this soft frosting provides a rich, tropical flavor, and the flaked coconut adds crunch. This frosting is an especially delicious addition to any chocolate cake.

1 can (15 ounces) cream of coconut
4 ounces (½ 8-ounce package) cream cheese, at room temperature
¼ cup (½ stick) unsalted butter, at room temperature
1 cup confectioners' sugar
1 cup sweetened flaked coconut

1. Mix cream of coconut, cream cheese, and butter together in a mixer on medium-low speed until smoothly blended.

2. Add sugar, ½ cup at a time, and mix until smooth. Stir in flaked coconut.

3. Cover and refrigerate for at least 1 hour before frosting cake. Keep frosted cake in a cool place until ready to serve.

CAKES SUGGESTED FOR THIS FROSTING

*Chocolate Layer Cake
*Classic or Chocolate Sponge Cake
*Banana Bundt Cake
Carrot Cake
Spice Cake

Apricot Cheese Frosting

Yield: 3½ cups

This soft, tawny colored frosting is flecked with apricot preserves. Orange extract helps to further accentuate the apricot flavor.

1 package (8 ounces) cream cheese, at room temperature
1 cup ricotta cheese
1 jar (10 ounces) apricot preserves
½ teaspoon orange extract
¾ cup confectioners' sugar

1. Combine cream cheese and ricotta in the bowl of a mixer. Beat on medium speed until soft. Add preserves and orange extract. Mix until smooth.
2. Add sugar, ¼ cup at a time, and mix until well blended.
3. Use immediately to frost cake, or cover and refrigerate until ready to use.

CAKES SUGGESTED FOR THIS FROSTING

*Basic Butter Cake (White or Yellow)
*Chocolate Layer Cake
Carrot Cake
Spice Cake

Cranberry Cream Cheese Frosting

Yield: 3 cups

A holiday frosting that provides a festive cover for plain cakes. Use sugared mint leaves to add a decorative trim (see Index, "Sugared Fruit, Mint Leaves, and Flower Petals").

1 package (8 ounces) cream cheese, at room temperature
1 cup canned jellied cranberry sauce
1½ cups confectioners' sugar

1. Beat cream cheese in a mixer on medium speed until creamed.
2. Add cranberry sauce and beat until blended.
3. Reduce mixer speed to medium low and add sugar, ½ cup at a time. Blend until smooth.
4. Use immediately to frost cake, or cover and refrigerate until ready to use.

CAKES SUGGESTED FOR THIS FROSTING

*Basic Butter Cake (White or Yellow)
*Applesauce Bundt Cake
Sour Cream Cake
Pecan or Walnut Cake

Cannoli Frosting

Yield: 2½ cups

Everyone who has tasted the sweet ricotta cheese filling inside crunchy cannoli shells loves it. This delightful variation takes the creamy, chocolate-flecked Sicilian treat out of the shell and spreads it over a moist, butter-rich cake. Don't anticipate any leftovers.

2 cups ricotta cheese
1½ cups confectioners' sugar
½ teaspoon ground cinnamon
1 ounce semisweet chocolate

1. Cream the cheese in a mixer on medium speed until smooth.
2. Reduce mixer speed to medium low and add sugar, scraping down sides of bowl with rubber spatula as necessary. Add cinnamon. Stop mixing when blended. Set bowl aside.
3. Using the coarse-shred side of a hand-held grater, shred the chocolate into shavings over a piece of waxed paper. Add shavings to ricotta mixture and stir by hand until well mixed.
4. Use immediately to frost cake, or cover and refrigerate for up to 2 days before using.

CAKES SUGGESTED FOR THIS FROSTING

*Chocolate Layer Cake
*Basic Butter Cake (White or Yellow)
*Classic or Chocolate Sponge Cake (Layer or Roll)
Spice Cake

Lemon Cream Frosting

Yield: 2½ cups

Intensely lemon flavored yet sweetly satisfying, this cream frosting will melt in your mouth.

½ cup granulated sugar
1 teaspoon grated lemon rind (1 lemon)
½ cup freshly squeezed lemon juice (2 lemons)
¼ cup (½ stick) unsalted butter, cut into tablespoon-size
    pieces
1 cup whipping cream
¾ cup confectioners' sugar

1. Combine sugar, lemon rind, and juice in a small saucepan. Bring to a boil over medium heat, stirring until sugar dissolves. Boil 5 minutes and remove from heat.
2. Immediately add the butter pieces and stir until melted. Pour into a bowl and set aside at room temperature to cool. (You can make this ahead, cover, and set aside at room temperature. Proceed with the third step when convenient.)
3. Whip cream in a mixer on medium-low speed until thickened. Add confectioners' sugar and beat until soft peaks form. Still beating, add the cooled lemon mixture. Continue to beat until soft peaks form again.
4. Use immediately to frost cake, or cover and refrigerate for up to 2 days before using. Keep frosted cake in a cool place until ready to serve.

CAKES SUGGESTED FOR THIS FROSTING

*Basic Butter Cake (White or Yellow)
*Classic Sponge Cake (Layer or Roll)
Gingerbread
Almond Cake

Velvety Chocolate Frosting

Yield: 3 cups

Melted chocolate combined with cream cheese lends new meaning to the word *velvet*. This smooth-textured frosting will practically spread itself.

4 ounces unsweetened chocolate
1 package (8 ounces) cream cheese, at room temperature
¼ cup cooled coffee
2 teaspoons vanilla extract
3 cups confectioners' sugar

1. Cut chocolate into small pieces and place in a glass bowl. Microwave on high power until chocolate is almost melted, about 1½ minutes. Remove from microwave oven and stir until completely melted. Or melt chocolate in a double boiler over barely simmering water (see Index, "How to Melt Chocolate").

2. Beat cream cheese in a mixer on medium-low speed until smooth. Add melted chocolate. Then add coffee and vanilla.

3. Begin adding sugar, ½ cup at a time, scraping down mixture with a rubber spatula as necessary. Increase mixer speed to medium and beat 30 seconds longer until smooth.

4. Use immediately to frost cake, or cover and refrigerate until ready to use.

CAKES SUGGESTED FOR THIS FROSTING

★Chocolate Layer Cake
★Basic Butter Cake (White or Yellow)

Sweet-Chocolate Cloud Frosting

Yield: 2½ cups

The sweet-chocolate flavor lingers after each bite of this cloud-soft frosting. It has only two ingredients and takes only minutes to prepare.

8 ounces (2 bars) sweet chocolate
1 cup whipping cream

1. Cut chocolate into small pieces and place in a glass bowl. Microwave on high power until chocolate is almost melted, about 1½ minutes. Remove from microwave oven and stir until completely melted. Or melt chocolate in a double boiler over barely simmering water (see Index, "How to Melt Chocolate"). Set aside.

2. Whip cream in a mixer on medium speed (or by hand with a whisk) until soft peaks form. Remove bowl from mixer. Pour in melted chocolate and whip by hand with a whisk until stiff peaks form. (If you use an electric beater instead of a whisk you risk overbeating the cream before the chocolate is blended in.)

3. Use immediately to frost cake. (Do not refrigerate, as this frosting sets very firm.) Keep frosted cake in a cool place until ready to serve.

Garnish tip: Decorate cake with chocolate shavings (see Index, "Cannoli Frosting," Step 3).

CAKES SUGGESTED FOR THIS FROSTING

*Chocolate Layer Cake
*Basic Butter Cake (White or Yellow)
Marble Cake

Better-than-Fudge Frosting

Yield: 3 cups

As the title suggests, this frosting is so rich and good that it may never make it to the cake. Because there are so few ingredients, a high-quality chocolate makes a big difference in taste.

1 pound semisweet chocolate
¾ cup whipping cream
⅓ cup (5½ tablespoons) unsalted butter,
*   cut into tablespoon-size pieces*
1 tablespoon vanilla extract

1. Cut chocolate into small pieces and place in the bowl of a mixer.
2. Combine cream and butter in a small saucepan. Bring to a full boil over medium heat. Remove from heat, pour over chocolate, and begin mixing on medium-low speed until chocolate is melted. Add vanilla and mix until smoothly blended.
3. Let frosting cool until thickened to spreading consistency before frosting cake (frosting may be refrigerated up to 1 hour).

CAKES SUGGESTED FOR THIS FROSTING

*Basic Butter Cake (White or Yellow)
*Chocolate Layer Cake
*Banana Bundt Cake
*Classic or Chocolate Sponge Cake (Layer or Roll)

Chocolate-Orange Frosting

Yield: 2⅔ cups

The sweet and tangy taste of this frosting is perfect for orange or chocolate cake. A garnish of glazed orange peel adds a slightly bitter crunch.

4 ounces semisweet chocolate
½ cup (1 stick) unsalted butter, at room temperature
3 cups confectioners' sugar
½ cup orange juice

1. Cut chocolate into small pieces and place in a glass bowl. Microwave on high power until chocolate is almost melted, about 1½ minutes. Remove from microwave oven and stir until completely melted. Or melt chocolate in a double boiler over barely simmering water (see Index, "How to Melt Chocolate"). Set aside.

2. Cream butter in a mixer on low speed until soft. Add melted chocolate and blend.

3. Add 1½ cups of the sugar (mixture will be very thick) and then add the orange juice while mixing on low speed. Add remaining sugar and increase mixer speed to medium until ingredients are smoothly blended.

4. Use immediately to frost cake, or cover and set aside at room temperature for up to 4 hours before using.

Garnish tip: Decorate cake with glazed orange peel (see Index, "Glazed Citrus Peel").

CAKES SUGGESTED FOR THIS FROSTING

*Chocolate Layer Cake
*Basic Butter Cake (White or Yellow)
*Banana Bundt Cake
Orange Cake

Chocolate-Peanut Butter Frosting

Yield: 2½ cups

Every child's dream come true! Delicious, thick chocolate blended with creamy peanut butter is an unbeatable combination. Use it to top a favorite cake for a party.

1 cup creamy peanut butter
½ cup packed light brown sugar
12 ounces (1 package) real semisweet chocolate chips
2 teaspoons vanilla extract

1. Combine peanut butter and sugar in the bowl of a mixer. Mix just until blended.
2. Place chocolate chips in a glass bowl. Microwave on high power until chocolate is almost melted, about 2 minutes. Remove from microwave oven and stir until completely melted. Or melt chocolate in a double boiler over barely simmering water (see Index, "How to Melt Chocolate").
3. Immediately pour the melted chocolate over the peanut butter mixture and begin mixing on low speed until blended. Add vanilla and increase mixer speed to medium. Beat until smooth and shiny, about 2 minutes.
4. Use immediately to frost cake, or cover and set aside at room temperature until ready to use.

CAKES (OR CUPCAKES) SUGGESTED FOR THIS FROSTING

*Chocolate Layer Cake
*Basic Butter Cake (White or Yellow)
*Banana Bundt Cake
Marble Cake

Chocolate-Chestnut Frosting

Yield: 3 cups

The deep, rich, chestnut flavor of this treat is complemented by sweet, melted chocolate. Use a light hand when applying this frosting, as a little goes a long way.

6 ounces semisweet chocolate
1½ cups canned unsweetened chestnut puree
1½ tablespoons vanilla extract
3 cups confectioners' sugar

1. Cut chocolate into small pieces and place in a glass bowl. Microwave on high power until chocolate is almost melted, about 1½ minutes. Remove from microwave oven and stir until completely melted. Or melt chocolate in a double boiler over barely simmering water (see Index, "How to Melt Chocolate"). Set aside.

2. Combine chestnut puree and vanilla in a mixer. Mix on medium-low speed 30 seconds to blend.

3. Add melted chocolate and blend. Begin adding sugar, ½ cup at a time, scraping down sides of bowl as necessary. When all sugar has been added, increase mixer speed to medium high and beat to blend smoothly.

4. Use immediately, or cover and refrigerate until ready to use.

CAKES SUGGESTED FOR THIS FROSTING

*Basic Butter Cake (White or Yellow)
*Chocolate Layer Cake
Spice Cake

White-Chocolate Dream Frosting

Yield: 3 cups

It is imperative that high-quality white chocolate be used in this truly wonderful frosting. Read the package label to be sure that cocoa butter is an ingredient. If there is no cocoa butter, you are purchasing candy and not white chocolate. This frosting is made ahead and refrigerated for later use.

9 ounces (3 3-ounce bars) white chocolate
4 ounces (½ 8-ounce package) cream cheese
¾ cup whipping cream

⅓ cup (5⅓ tablespoons) unsalted butter,
*   cut into tablespoon-size pices*
½ teaspoon almond extract
¾ cup confectioners' sugar

1. Cut white chocolate and cream cheese into small pieces. Combine in the bowl of a mixer.
2. Combine cream and butter in a small saucepan. Bring to a full boil over medium heat.
3. With mixer running on low speed, immediately pour hot cream mixture over white chocolate mixture. When blended, add almond extract.
4. Add sugar, scraping sides of bowl as necessary. Increase speed to medium until mixture is smoothly blended. (Mixture will be thin.)
5. Pour into a bowl, cover, and refrigerate until stiffened to a spreadable consistency, at least 4 hours. Stir before frosting cake.

Garnish tip: Add crunch to your frosted cake with either Toasted Coconut, Macadamia Nut Brittle, or Sugar-and-Spice Nut Crunch (see Index).

CAKES SUGGESTED FOR THIS FROSTING

*Basic Butter Cake (White or Yellow)
*Chocolate Layer Cake
*Classic or Chocolate Sponge Cake (Layer or Roll)
Spice Cake
Almond Cake

Southern Meringue Fluff Frosting

Yield: 4 cups

This meringue-style frosting gets its warm beige hue from dark molasses. Rum extract supplies just a hint of intrigue.

2 large egg whites
1 cup granulated sugar
¼ cup water
2 tablespoons dark molasses
¼ teaspoon cream of tartar
1 teaspoon rum extract

1. Pour 2 inches of water into a large saucepan and bring the water to a simmer over low heat. Meanwhile, combine egg whites, sugar, ¼ cup water, molasses, and cream of tartar in the bowl of a mixer. Stir by hand with a whisk to blend. Place bowl in the pan of simmering water. Continue to whisk until sugar is dissolved and mixture feels warm, but not hot, to the touch. Remove bowl from the heat and begin mixing in the electric mixer on medium speed.

2. Mix until lightened in color and thickened, about 4 minutes. Add rum extract, increase mixer speed to high, and beat to stiff peaks, about 2 minutes.

3. Use immediately to frost cake. Set frosted cake aside at room temperature until ready to serve.

CAKES SUGGESTED FOR THIS FROSTING

*Basic Butter Cake (White or Yellow)
Spice Cake
Carrot Cake
Rum Cake

Marshmallow Frosting

Yield: 3½ cups

This fluffy frosting is as white as snow and just as soft. Apply to your cake lavishly, spreading swirls and peaks to make a thick coat of candylike topping.

3 cups (½ 10½-ounce bag) miniature marshmallows
½ cup light corn syrup
2 large egg whites
½ teaspoon cream of tartar

1. Combine marshmallows and corn syrup in a medium-size glass bowl. Microwave on high power until the marshmallows are almost melted, about 1½ minutes. Remove from microwave oven and stir until completely melted. Or melt in a double boiler over simmering water, stirring occasionally.

2. Combine egg whites and cream of tartar in a mixing bowl. Beat on medium speed until stiff peaks form. Pour melted marshmallow mixture into whites while still beating. Increase mixer speed to high and beat to stiff peaks, about 1 minute.

3. Use immediately to frost cake. Set frosted cake aside at room temperature until ready to serve.

Garnish tip: Before frosting dries, sprinkle with crushed candy or colored sprinkles.

CAKES SUGGESTED FOR THIS FROSTING

*Chocolate Layer Cake
*Banana Bundt Cake
*Basic Butter Cake (White or Yellow)

Peppermint Candy Frosting

Yield: 4 cups

Dense chocolate cake is the ideal pairing for this airy whipped frosting. Add a crushed candy garnish for lively texture contrast and spots of color.

2 large egg whites
1½ cups granulated sugar
¼ cup water
2 tablespoons light corn syrup
¼ teaspoon cream of tartar
½ teaspoon peppermint extract

1. Pour 2 inches of water into a large saucepan and bring the water to a simmer over low heat. Meanwhile, combine egg whites, sugar, ¼ cup water, corn syrup, and cream of tartar in the bowl of a mixer. Stir by hand with a whisk to blend. Place bowl in the pan of simmering water. Continue to whisk until sugar is dissolved and mixture feels warm, but not hot, to the touch. Remove bowl from the heat and begin mixing in the electric mixer on medium speed.

2. Mix until lightened in color and thickened, about 4 minutes. Add peppermint extract, increase mixer speed to high, and beat to stiff peaks, about 2 minutes.

3. Use immediately to frost cake. Set frosted cake aside at room temperature until ready to serve.

Garnish tip: Sprinkle with crushed peppermint candy before frosting dries.

CAKES SUGGESTED FOR THIS FROSTING

*Chocolate Layer Cake
*Basic Butter Cake (White or Yellow)
Devil's Food Cake

Coffee Buttercream Frosting

Buttercream is the queen of frostings—nothing tastes, looks, or spreads quite like it. This beaten egg-white method is easy and should take no longer than 15 minutes to prepare.

1 cup (2 sticks) unsalted butter
2 tablespoons instant espresso coffee granules
1 tablespoon hot water
3 large egg whites
1 cup superfine sugar

1. Cut butter into ½-inch pieces. Combine coffee and hot water in a small bowl and stir to dissolve the coffee. Set both aside.

2. Pour 2 inches of water into a large saucepan and bring the water to a simmer over low heat. Meanwhile, combine egg whites and sugar in the bowl of a mixer and stir by hand with a whisk to blend. Place bowl in the pan of simmering water. Continue to whisk until mixture feels warm, but not hot, to the touch. Remove bowl from the heat and begin mixing in an electric mixer on medium speed.

3. Within a couple of minutes, the whites will look shiny and thick. Begin adding butter piece by piece in a continuous feed. The mixture will begin to look like butter when approximately three-fourths of the butter has been added. Finish adding the butter, and then add the reserved coffee. Mix until thoroughly blended.

4. Use immediately to frost cake, or cover and refrigerate until ready to use. This frosting can also be frozen for up to 1 month. Return chilled frosting to room temperature before using.

Note: If this mixture curdles at the point when three-fourths of the butter has been added, simply increase mixer speed to high for 1 minute or until a creamy consistency returns. Then continue adding remaining butter at medium speed.

Garnish tip: Decorate cake rim with chocolate coffee beans.

CAKES SUGGESTED FOR THIS FROSTING

*Chocolate Layer Cake
*Classic or Chocolate Sponge Cake (Layer or Roll)
*Basic Butter Cake (White or Yellow)
Pecan or Walnut Cake

Praline Buttercream Frosting

Yield: 3 cups

Prepare the Praline ahead of time to make assembly of this buttercream a snap. The Praline provides a memorable caramelized-candy crunch.

1 cup (2 sticks) unsalted butter
½ cup Praline (see Index)
¼ cup pure maple syrup
3 large egg whites
⅔ cup superfine sugar

1. Cut butter into ½-inch pieces. Combine Praline and syrup in a small bowl and stir to mix. Set both aside.

2. Pour 2 inches of water into a large saucepan and bring the water to a simmer over low heat. Meanwhile, combine egg whites and sugar in the bowl of a mixer and stir by hand with a whisk to blend. Place bowl in the pan of simmering water. Continue to whisk until mixture feels warm, but not hot, to the touch. Remove bowl from the heat and begin mixing in an electric mixer on medium speed.

3. Within a couple of minutes, the whites will look shiny and thick. Begin adding butter piece by piece in a continuous feed. The mixture will begin to look like butter when approximately three-fourths of the butter has been added. Finish adding butter, and then add reserved Praline-syrup mixture. Blend thoroughly.

4. Use immediately to frost cake, or cover and refrigerate until ready to use. This frosting can also be frozen for up to 1 month. Return chilled frosting to room temperature before using.

Note: If frosting curdles, refer to Note at end of "Coffee Buttercream Frosting" recipe (see Index).

Garnish tip: Sprinkle cake top with Praline (see Index).

CAKES SUGGESTED FOR THIS FROSTING

*Classic or Chocolate Sponge Cake (Layer or Roll)
*Basic Butter Cake (White or Yellow)
Spice Cake
Rum Cake

Raspberry Buttercream Frosting

Yield: 3 cups

This is a terrific filling for Sponge Cake Roll (see Index). Be sure to use raspberry jam and not preserves for this buttercream, as the preserves are full of seeds.

1 cup (2 sticks) unsalted butter
½ cup raspberry jam
1 tablespoon freshly squeezed lemon juice
3 large egg whites
⅔ cup superfine sugar

1. Cut butter into ½-inch pieces. Combine jam and lemon juice in a small bowl and stir to mix. Set both aside.
2. Pour 2 inches of water into a large saucepan and bring the water to a simmer over low heat. Meanwhile, combine egg whites and sugar in the bowl of a mixer and stir by hand with a whisk to blend. Place bowl in the pan of simmering water. Continue to whisk until mixture feels warm, but not hot, to the touch. Remove bowl from the heat and begin mixing in an electric mixer on medium speed.
3. Within a couple of minutes, the whites will look shiny and thick. Begin adding butter piece by piece in a continuous feed. The mixture will begin to look like butter when approximately three-fourths of the butter has been added. Finish adding butter, and then add reserved raspberry mixture. Blend thoroughly.
4. Use immediately to frost cake, or cover and refrigerate until ready to use. This frosting can also be frozen for up to 1 month. Return chilled frosting to room temperature before using.

Note: If frosting curdles, refer to Note at end of "Coffee Buttercream Frosting" recipe (see Index).

Garnish tip: Decorate cake top with fresh raspberries or sugared rose petals (see Index, "Sugared Fruit, Mint Leaves, and Flower Petals").

CAKES SUGGESTED FOR THIS FROSTING

*Classic or Chocolate Sponge Cake (Layer or Roll)
*Basic Butter Cake (White or Yellow)
*Chocolate Layer Cake
Buttermilk or Sour Cream Cake
Meringue Layer Cake

Orange Buttercream Frosting

Yield: 3 cups

Freshly grated orange rind is this recipe's distinguishing feature. It gives the buttercream a fresh orange flavor and attractive flecked texture.

1 cup (2 sticks) unsalted butter
3 tablespoons orange liqueur
1 tablespoon grated orange rind (1 orange)
3 large egg whites
1 cup superfine sugar

1. Cut butter into ½-inch pieces. Combine liqueur and orange rind in a small bowl and stir to mix. Set both aside.

2. Pour 2 inches of water into a large saucepan and bring the water to a simmer over low heat. Meanwhile, combine egg whites and sugar in the bowl of a mixer and stir by hand with a whisk to blend. Place bowl in the pan of simmering water. Continue to whisk until mixture feels warm, but not hot, to the touch. Remove bowl from the heat and begin mixing in an electric mixer on medium speed.

3. Within a couple of minutes, the whites will look shiny and thick. Begin adding butter piece by piece in a continuous feed. The mixture will begin to look like butter when approximately three-fourths of the butter has been added. Finish adding butter, and then add reserved orange mixture. Blend thoroughly.

4. Use immediately to frost cake, or cover and refrigerate until ready to use. This frosting can also be frozen for up to 1 month. Return chilled frosting to room temperature before using.

Note: If frosting curdles, refer to Note at end of "Coffee Buttercream Frosting" recipe (see Index).

CAKES SUGGESTED FOR THIS FROSTING

*Basic Butter Cake (White or Yellow)
*Chocolate Layer Cake
*Classic or Chocolate Sponge Cake (Layer or Roll)
Orange Cake

Bittersweet Chocolate Buttercream Frosting

Yield: 3 cups

Bittersweet chocolate is used to flavor this fluffy, soft buttercream. You could also use your favorite brand of unsweetened chocolate.

1 cup (2 sticks) unsalted butter
2 ounces bittersweet chocolate
3 large egg whites
1 cup superfine sugar

1. Cut butter into ½-inch pieces. Set aside. Cut chocolate into small pieces and place in a glass bowl. Microwave on high power until chocolate is almost melted, about 1½ minutes. Remove from microwave oven and stir until completely melted. Or melt chocolate in a double boiler over barely simmering water (see Index, "How to Melt Chocolate"). Set aside.

2. Pour 2 inches of water into a large saucepan and bring the water to a simmer over low heat. Meanwhile, combine egg whites and sugar in the bowl of a mixer and stir by hand with a whisk to blend. Place bowl in the pan of simmering water. Continue to whisk until mixture feels warm, but not hot, to the touch. Remove bowl from the heat and begin mixing in an electric mixer on medium speed.

3. Within a couple of minutes, the whites will look shiny and thick. Begin adding butter piece by piece in a continuous feed. The mixture will begin to look like butter when approximately three-fourths of the butter has been added. Finish adding butter, and then add melted chocolate. Mix until thoroughly blended.

4. Use immediately to frost cake, or cover and refrigerate until ready to use. This frosting can also be frozen for up to 1 month. Return chilled frosting to room temperature before using.

Note: If frosting curdles, refer to Note at end of "Coffee Buttercream Frosting" recipe (see Index.)

Garnish tip: Decorate cake with chocolate curls or leaves (see Index, "Chocolate Shapes and Curls" and "Chocolate-Coated Fruit and Leaves").

CAKES SUGGESTED FOR THIS FROSTING

*Chocolate Layer Cake
*Classic or Chocolate Sponge Cake (Layer or Roll)
*Basic Butter Cake (White or Yellow)
Sour Cream Cake
Almond Cake

8
Fillings

Who can resist the sensation of biting into the creamy sweetness of a moist, flavorful filled cake? This chapter and those that follow will provide you with various intriguing alternatives for dressing up any cake.

A filled sponge cake roll requires no extra embellishment. A filled layer cake does, and it can be decorated in several eye-catching ways.

First, apply filling between cake layers. Next, clean up the outside rim of the filled layers by running the edge of a thin metal spatula around the cake sides. A smooth, thin coating of the filling can then be applied to the cake sides with the spatula. Now add a decorative garnish. As a final touch, sprinkle the cake top with confectioners' sugar or cocoa powder.

Instead of decorating just the sides of the cake, you can trim the top only or both the top and sides. Clean up the outside rim of the filled layers as described above. Then apply a smooth, thin coating of the filling to the cake top. Sprinkle (or place) a garnish on the top until it is evenly covered. See Chapter 12 for recipes and other ideas.

Another way to give your filled layer cake a finished look is to select an icing or glaze that complements the filling, such as lemon icing or caramel glaze with raspberry mousse filling, or banana icing or chocolate glaze with mocha mousse filling. See Chapter 9 for recipes and other ideas.

Note: You will need 3 cups of filling for one sponge cake roll; 1½ cups of filling are sufficient for a layer cake.

This symbol, *, used in front of the name of a cake, means that the cake recipe can be found in this book.

Honey Butter Filling

Yield: 3 cups

Lip-smacking good! Keep a little on hand for your morning toast.

1½ cups (3 sticks) unsalted butter, at room temperature
¾ cup honey
¾ cup confectioners' sugar

1. Cream butter in a bowl until soft. Add honey and sugar and blend until smooth.

2. Use immediately or set aside at room temperature until ready to use. Store covered in refrigerator for up to 2 weeks. Return to room temperature before using.

CAKES SUGGESTED FOR THIS FILLING

*Classic or Chocolate Sponge Cake (Layer or Roll)
*Basic Butter Cake (White or Yellow)
*Chocolate Layer Cake

Almond Cream Filling

Yield: 3 cups

Nutty and mildly sweet, this filling is far superior to the canned version found in supermarkets.

1 cup (2 sticks) unsalted butter, at room temperature
2 cups (8 ounces) finely ground almonds
2 large egg whites
½ teaspoon almond extract
2 cups confectioners' sugar

1. Cream butter in a bowl until soft. Add almonds, egg whites, and almond extract. Blend until smooth.

2. Add sugar, ½ cup at a time, until well mixed. Beat vigorously for 30 seconds to thoroughly blend ingredients.

3. Use immediately or set aside at room temperature until ready to use. Store covered in refrigerator for up to 2 weeks. Return to room temperature before using.

CAKES SUGGESTED FOR THIS FILLING

*Classic or Chocolate Sponge Cake (Layer or Roll)
*Basic Butter Cake (White or Yellow)
*Chocolate Layer Cake

Whipped Cream Filling

Yield: 4 cups

Whipped cream is pure, classic, and totally irresistible. As good as it is, however, plain whipped cream is too light and delicate to be used as cake filling. This version adds a touch of gelatin for firmness. It is ideal for frosting cakes as well.

1 envelope unflavored gelatin
2 tablespoons cool water
2 cups whipping cream
½ cup confectioners' sugar
1 teaspoon vanilla extract

1. Sprinkle gelatin over cool water in a small glass bowl. Let stand 1 minute to set. Microwave on high power to melt and warm for 30 seconds. Or add the gelatin to the water in a small saucepan, and then melt over low heat until warmed (do not boil). Remove from the heat and set aside to cool slightly.

2. Whip cream in mixer on medium speed until it just begins to thicken. Add the sugar and vanilla. Beat until softly whipped, but not stiff. Still beating, add the cooled, but still liquid, gelatin to the cream. Beat just until stiff peaks form.

3. Use immediately or cover and refrigerate for up to 1 day before using. Keep filled or frosted cake in a cool place until ready to serve.

CAKES SUGGESTED FOR THIS FILLING

*Classic or Chocolate Sponge Cake (Layer or Roll)
*Chocolate Layer Cake
*Basic Butter Cake (White or Yellow)

Raspberry Mousse Filling

Yield: 3½ cups

This pretty pink filling has an exceptionally intense berry flavor. Use it in a cake for your sweetheart on Valentine's Day.

1 package (10 ounces) frozen sweetened raspberries
1 envelope unflavored gelatin
¼ cup raspberry or cherry liqueur (or light rum)
1 cup whipping cream
3 tablespoons confectioners' sugar

1. Puree frozen berries in an electric blender. Transfer to a glass bowl or a saucepan.

2. Sprinkle gelatin over the liqueur in a small bowl. Let stand 1 minute to set. Stir into the berry puree.

3. Microwave berry mixture in a bowl on high power until warm, about 3 minutes. Or heat mixture in saucepan until warm, but not hot. Set aside to cool to room temperature.

4. Whip cream with the sugar until soft peaks form. Fold the raspberry mixture into the cream.

5. Cover and refrigerate until set, about 1 hour. Use within 2 days. Keep filled cake in a cool place until ready to serve.

CAKES SUGGESTED FOR THIS FILLING

*Classic or Chocolate Sponge Cake (Layer or Roll)
*Basic Butter Cake (White or Yellow)
*Chocolate Layer Cake

Mocha Mousse Filling

Yield: 3 cups

Coffee and cocoa lovers will swoon over this combination of the two delicious flavors. Rolled up in Chocolate Sponge Cake, this filling makes for an especially festive finale to a winter holiday meal.

2 large egg whites
1 envelope unflavored gelatin
1 tablespoon instant coffee granules
1 tablespoon unsweetened cocoa powder
¼ cup coffee liqueur
½ cup granulated sugar
1 cup whipping cream

1. Pour 2 inches of water into a large saucepan and bring the water to a simmer over low heat. Place egg whites in the bowl of a mixer. Sprinkle gelatin over whites and let stand 1 minute.

2. Meanwhile, combine coffee, cocoa powder, and liqueur in a small bowl. Stir to blend and dissolve coffee. Stir this mixture into the egg white mixture.

3. Place bowl in the pan of simmering water. Whisk until mixture feels hot to the touch. Remove bowl from the heat and begin mixing in an electric mixer on medium-high speed.

4. Add the sugar and beat until thoroughly blended, about 2 minutes. Set aside at room temperature until mixture begins to set, about 5 minutes.

5. Whip cream until soft peaks form. Fold the coffee mixture into the cream.

6. Use immediately or cover and refrigerate for up to 1 day before using. Keep filled cake in a cool place until ready to serve.

CAKES SUGGESTED FOR THIS FILLING

*Classic or Chocolate Sponge Cake (Layer or Roll)
*Chocolate Layer Cake
*Basic Butter Cake (White or Yellow)

9
Icings and Glazes

Icings and glazes are two types of coatings, with icings generally being thicker and sweeter than glazes. Icings are quick to prepare and can be created at the last minute from even a minimally stocked pantry. Most icings are applied to the cake immediately after they are prepared. Glazes give a smooth sheen and finish to cakes and lend an extra flavor dimension. One can even spread a frosting over a glaze, if desired.

Icings, in their simplest form, are a combination of confectioners' sugar and liquid, such as milk or lemon juice. They can be thinned by adding more liquid or thickened by holding some liquid back. They will set on the cake quickly and harden as the sugar dries. Glazes will set also but will not harden because they contain less sugar. Any garnish—such as toasted pecans (see Index) or Glazed Citrus Peel (see Index)—should be applied while icing or glaze is wet.

To apply icing or glaze, position a completely cooled cake on a wire rack over aluminum foil or waxed paper to catch drips. Spoon or pour a generous amount of icing or glaze over the center of the cake, then allow gravity to spread it over the top and down the sides of the cake in cascading drips. Use the back of a spoon or a thin spatula to spread icing or glaze over thin areas and into empty spaces. Repeat the application until the cake is well coated. Stop spreading once the icing or glaze begins to set so that the smooth finish will not be lost. (Don't worry, you have several minutes before icing begins to set.) When set, transfer the cake to a serving platter. One cup of icing or glaze is sufficient for one bundt, tube, or loaf cake.

This symbol, *, used in front of the name of a cake, means that the cake recipe can be found in this book.

Lemon Icing

Yield: 1 cup

Opposites do indeed attract! Here, sweet sugar and tart lemon are combined to create this simplest (and one of the best) of all icings. If a thicker icing is desired, simply reduce the amount of lemon juice.

2 cups confectioners' sugar
¼ cup freshly squeezed lemon juice (1 lemon)

1. Place sugar in a bowl. Whisk in the lemon juice until smoothly blended. Set aside for 5 minutes to set slightly.
2. Spoon a generous amount over cake center, allowing icing to spread and flow down sides of cake. Repeat, using all the icing, or stop when desired amount has adhered.
3. When icing has set and dried, transfer cake to a serving platter.

Garnish tip: Decorate with glazed lemon peel before the icing dries (see Index, "Glazed Citrus Peel").

CAKES SUGGESTED FOR THIS ICING

*(Not Quite So) Plain or Lemon Pound Cake
*Applesauce or Banana Bundt Cake
Spice Cake
Gingerbread
Carrot Cake

Ginger Icing

Yield: 1 cup

Exotic and aggressively flavored, this icing has a peppery, spicy taste that lingers on after each bite. Try it on cakes made with cream, lemon, or tropical fruit for a particularly good flavor match.

3 tablespoons milk
1 tablespoon preserved stem ginger syrup (see Note)
½ teaspoon ground ginger
2 cups confectioners' sugar
2 pieces preserved stem ginger, cut into slivers (see Note)

1. Combine milk, syrup, and ground ginger in a bowl. Using a whisk, blend the ingredients. Add sugar, ½ cup at a time, whisking until smooth. Set aside for 5 minutes to set slightly.

2. Spoon a generous amount over cake center, allowing icing to spread and flow down sides of cake. Repeat, using all the icing, or stop when desired amount has adhered.

3. When icing has set and dried, transfer cake to a serving platter.

4. Decorate cake top with ginger slivers (use a zigzag pattern) before the icing dries.

Note: Preserved stem ginger in syrup is sold in jars in specialty food sections of supermarkets. If unavailable, substitute 1 tablespoon sugar syrup (recipe follows) for the ginger syrup and 2 tablespoons finely chopped candied ginger for the stem ginger slivers. Scatter the candied ginger over the wet icing.

To make sugar syrup, boil 2 tablespoons granulated sugar with 1 tablespoon water just until sugar dissolves (less than a minute) and cool before using.

CAKES SUGGESTED FOR THIS ICING

★(Not Quite So) Plain or Lemon Pound Cake
★Applesauce or Banana Bundt Cake
Buttermilk or Sour Cream Cake
Coconut Cake

Rum-Butter Icing

Yield: 1 cup

Use an aged dark rum or the best light rum possible for this icing. The better the rum, the better the flavor of the icing.

¼ cup (½ stick) unsalted butter
3 tablespoons rum, preferably dark
1½ cups confectioners' sugar

1. Melt butter in the microwave oven on high power for 1 minute or on top of the stove. Stir rum and melted butter together in a bowl. Stir in sugar, ½ cup at a time, whisking until smooth.
2. Spoon a generous amount over cake center, allowing icing to spread and flow down sides of cake. Repeat, using all the icing, or stop when desired amount has adhered.
3. When icing has set and dried, transfer cake to a serving platter.

Garnish tip: Decorate with toasted pecan halves (see Index) before the icing dries.

CAKES SUGGESTED FOR THIS ICING

*(Not Quite So) Plain or Lemon Pound Cake
*Applesauce or Banana Bundt Cake
Pecan Cake
Spice Cake
Gingerbread

Banana Icing

Yield: 1⅓ cups

Soft, ripe banana adds delicate flavor and texture to this icing. Delicious on any number of cakes, it's especially good drizzled on a nut-laced coffee cake as well.

1 medium-size ripe banana
1 teaspoon fresh lemon juice
½ teaspoon banana extract
¼ cup (½ stick) unsalted butter, at room temperature
1½ cups confectioners' sugar

1. Mash banana with lemon juice and banana extract to a smooth puree. Set aside.
2. Cream butter in a mixer bowl on medium-low speed until smooth. Add banana mixture and sugar, ½ cup at a time, until smoothly blended.
3. Spoon a generous amount over cake center, allowing icing to spread and flow down sides of cake. Repeat, using all the icing, or stop when desired amount has adhered.
4. When icing has set and dried, transfer cake to a serving platter.

Garnish tip: Sprinkle top lightly with ground cinnamon.

CAKES SUGGESTED FOR THIS ICING

★(Not Quite So) Plain, Lemon, or Praline Pound Cake
★Applesauce or Banana Bundt Cake
Chocolate Bundt Cake
Peanut Butter Loaf Cake

Holiday Green Chartreuse Icing

Yield: 1 cup

Chartreuse, a french liqueur, flavored with many herbs, gives this icing a lovely, soft mint-green color. For a festive touch, spoon Whipped Blush Cream (see Index) over cake slices before serving.

¼ cup (½ stick) unsalted butter, at room temperature
1 large egg white
1 tablespoon green Chartreuse liqueur
1 drop green food color
1½ cups confectioners' sugar

1. Combine butter, egg white, liqueur, and green food color in the bowl of a mixer. Mix on medium-low speed to blend.
2. Add sugar, ½ cup at a time, blending until smooth. Scrape down ingredients with a rubber spatula as necessary.
3. Spoon a generous amount over cake center, allowing icing to spread and flow down sides of cake. Repeat, using all the icing, or stop when desired amount has adhered.
4. When icing has set and dried, transfer cake to a serving platter.

Garnish tip: An attractive decoration on this cake is colorful pieces of glacéed fruit, added while icing is still wet.

CAKES SUGGESTED FOR THIS ICING

*(Not Quite So) Plain or Lemon Pound Cake
*Applesauce or Banana Bundt Cake
Chocolate Bundt Cake
Sour Cream Bundt Cake

Tropical Fruit Glaze

Yield: ¾ cup

This clear, amber glaze gives a lustrous shine to a cake. Use it alone on a cake or brush it on before frosting the cake with buttercream or other creamy frosting. It keeps well, so double the recipe to have some on hand for cake-decorating emergencies.

6 ounces (½ 12-ounce can) frozen tropical fruit juice
*   concentrate, thawed*
2 tablespoons honey
1 tablespoon rum
2 teaspoons arrowroot or cornstarch

1. Combine thawed concentrate and honey in a small saucepan. Turn on heat to medium and bring the mixture to a boil while stirring. Boil 5 minutes.
2. Meanwhile, mix rum and arrowroot together in a small bowl. Add to fruit mixture, stir, and bring back to a boil. Remove from heat, set aside, and cool to room temperature before using.
3. Pour or spoon over cake, allowing glaze to flow down the sides. Reapply fallen drips with a spoon as necessary.
4. Let glaze on cake set for at least 1 hour before transferring cake to a serving platter.

Note: This glaze can be made ahead, covered, and stored at room temperature for up to 3 days.

CAKES SUGGESTED FOR THIS GLAZE

*(Not Quite So) Plain or Lemon Pound Cake
*Applesauce or Banana Bundt Cake
Coconut Cake
Orange Cake

Chocolate Glaze

Yield: 1 cup

Plan to use this icing immediately after preparation—it sets quickly as the chocolate cools.

6 ounces real semisweet chocolate chips
2 tablespoons unsalted butter, cut into small pieces
¼ cup light corn syrup

1. Combine chocolate chips and butter in a glass bowl. Microwave on high power until the chocolate is almost melted, about 1½ minutes. Remove from microwave oven and stir until completely melted. Or melt chocolate and butter in a double boiler over barely simmering water (see Index, "How to Melt Chocolate").

2. Stir in corn syrup until smoothly blended. Immediately pour or spread over cake, allowing glaze to flow down the sides.

3. Let glaze on cake set for at least 1 hour before transferring cake to a serving platter.

Garnish tip: Decorate with chocolate curls or chocolate leaves before the glaze sets (see Index, "Chocolate Shapes and Curls" and "Chocolate-Coated Fruit and Leaves").

CAKES SUGGESTED FOR THIS GLAZE

*(Not Quite So) Plain or Praline Pound Cake
*Banana Bundt Cake
*Chocolate Sponge Cake (Roll)
Buttermilk or Sour Cream Cake
Chocolate Bundt Cake

Coffee Liqueur Glaze

Yield: ¾ cup

If coffee is a favorite flavor, your mouth should begin watering when you think of this glaze coating the outside of a mocha-filled sponge cake roll (see Index, "Mocha Mousse Filling" and "Sponge Cake Roll").

¾ cup coffee liqueur
½ cup confectioners' sugar
2 tablespoons unsalted butter
1 tablespoon cornstarch

1. Combine liqueur, sugar, butter, and cornstarch in a saucepan. Turn on heat to medium and bring the mixture to a boil while stirring. Boil 5 minutes to burn off the alcohol and thicken the glaze. Remove from heat, set aside, and cool to room temperature.

2. Pour or spoon over cake, allowing glaze to flow down the sides. Reapply fallen drips with a spoon as necessary.

3. Let glaze on cake set for at least 1 hour before transferring cake to a serving platter.

Note: This glaze can be made ahead, covered, and kept at room temperature for up to 2 days or in the refrigerator for several weeks. Return to room temperature before using.

CAKES SUGGESTED FOR THIS GLAZE

★(Not Quite So) Plain or Praline Pound Cake
★Classic or Chocolate Sponge Cake (Roll)
★Banana Bundt Cake
Walnut Cake

Maple Syrup Glaze

Yield: 1 cup

Be sure to use pure maple syrup for this glaze. Do not substitute commercial pancake syrup—it is a completely different product and lacks the distinctive flavor that makes this glaze so delicious.

1 cup pure maple syrup
3 tablespoons unsalted butter
1 tablespoon cornstarch

1. Combine syrup, butter, and cornstarch in a saucepan. Turn on heat to medium and bring the mixture to a boil while stirring. Boil 5 minutes to thicken the glaze. Remove from heat, set aside, and cool to room temperature.
2. Pour or spoon over cake, allowing glaze to flow down the sides. Reapply fallen drips with a spoon as necessary.
3. Let glaze on cake set for at least 1 hour before transferring cake to a serving platter.

Note: This glaze can be made ahead, covered, and kept at room temperature for up to 2 days or in the refrigerator for several weeks. Return to room temperature before using.

CAKES SUGGESTED FOR THIS GLAZE

*(Not Quite So) Plain or Praline Pound Cake
*Applesauce or Banana Bundt Cake
*Classic Sponge Cake (Roll)
Pecan or Walnut Cake

Caramel Glaze

Yield: ¾ cup

An irresistible complement to any cake made with apples or nuts.

¼ cup (½ stick) unsalted butter
½ cup packed light brown sugar
⅓ cup whipping cream

1. Combine butter, sugar, and cream in a saucepan. Turn on heat to medium and bring the mixture to a boil while stirring. Boil 5 minutes to thicken. Remove from heat, set aside, and cool for 5 to 10 minutes.
2. Pour or spoon over cake, allowing glaze to flow down the sides. Reapply fallen drips with a spoon as necessary.
3. Let glaze on cake set for at least 1 hour before transferring cake to a serving platter.

Garnish tip: Decorate with toasted pecans or toasted walnuts (see Index) before the glaze sets.

CAKES SUGGESTED FOR THIS GLAZE

*Applesauce or Banana Bundt Cake
*(Not Quite So) Plain or Praline Pound Cake
Pecan or Walnut Cake
Fresh Apple Cake

10
Toppings

A topping might be considered a thickened dessert sauce. It's a wonderfully simple finish that can add color and contrasting flavors to any cake.

The following ten recipes are for toppings intended to accompany your cake in one of two ways: they can be spread atop the cake or spooned onto cake slices. Note: All of these toppings are too soft to be used as frostings or fillings.

The toppings made with whipped cream are to be used immediately or chilled and used within a day. The others can be made several days ahead as noted.

To spread a topping, spoon it onto the center of the cake and spread it outward with a thin metal spatula. Allow the topping to cascade down the sides naturally. Toppings made with whipped cream will stay firmly atop the cake. After spreading the topping, set the cake aside before cutting it into slices to allow the topping to set. Cakes spread with topping should be kept in a cool place or refrigerated if not served within a couple of hours.

This symbol, *, used in front of the name of a cake, means that the cake recipe can be found in this book.

Whipped Blush Cream Topping

Yield: 2 cups

This looks spectacular on a chocolate cake.

1 cup whipping cream
2 tablespoons confectioners' sugar
2 tablespoons grenadine syrup

1. Whip cream in mixer on medium speed until thickened. Add sugar and continue to beat until soft peaks form.
2. Add syrup and beat just until stiff.

CAKES SUGGESTED FOR THIS TOPPING

*Chocolate Layer Cake
*Classic or Chocolate Sponge Cake
*(Not Quite So) Plain Pound Cake
*Cheesecake
Almond Cake

Whipped Mint Cream Topping

Yield: 2 cups

The peppermint schnapps in this topping gives it a festively fragrant and appealing aroma.

1 cup whipping cream
4 tablespoons confectioners' sugar
2 tablespoons peppermint schnapps liqueur

1. Whip cream in mixer on medium speed until thickened. Add sugar and continue to beat until soft peaks form.
2. Add the liqueur and beat just until stiff.

Garnish tip: Decorate mint cream with sugared mint leaves (see Index, "Sugared Fruit, Mint Leaves, and Flower Petals").

CAKES SUGGESTED FOR THIS TOPPING

*Chocolate Layer Cake
*(Not Quite So) Plain Pound Cake
*Classic or Chocolate Sponge Cake
*Basic Butter Cake (White or Yellow)
Gingerbread
Angel Food Cake

Espresso Cream Topping

Yield: 2 cups

Bittersweet perfection. You'll want to add some to your coffee as well as to your cake.

2 tablespoons coffee liqueur
2 teaspoons instant espresso coffee granules
1 cup whipping cream
½ cup confectioners' sugar

1. Combine liqueur and instant coffee in a small bowl. Stir to dissolve the coffee. Set aside.

2. Whip cream in mixer on medium speed until thickened. Add sugar and the coffee mixture. Continue to beat until stiff.

CAKES SUGGESTED FOR THIS TOPPING

*Chocolate Layer Cake

*Classic or Chocolate Sponge Cake

*Cheesecake or Mocha Cheesecake

*(Not Quite So) Plain or Praline Pound Cake

Flourless Chocolate Cake

Cocoa Cream Topping

Yield: 3 cups

A cool concoction for lovers of hot chocolate.

⅓ cup granulated sugar
¼ cup unsweetened cocoa powder
1 tablespoon cornstarch
1 cup half-and-half or whole milk
2 teaspoons vanilla extract
1 cup whipping cream
⅓ cup confectioners' sugar

1. Combine sugar, cocoa powder, cornstarch, and half-and-half in a saucepan. Turn on heat to medium and stir until mixture thickens and one or two bubbles appear on the surface (do not boil). Remove from heat.

2. Pour into a bowl and stir in vanilla. Cover the surface with waxed paper to prevent a skin from forming and refrigerate until cooled.

3. Whip cream in mixer on medium speed until thickened. Add confectioners' sugar and continue to beat until soft peaks form. Fold the cooled cocoa mixture into the cream mixture until blended. Spread over top of cooled cake before slicing, or spoon onto cake slices before serving.

Note: This topping can be made ahead, covered, and refrigerated for up to 1 day before using.

CAKES SUGGESTED FOR THIS TOPPING

*Chocolate Layer Cake
*Basic Butter Cake (White or Yellow)
*(Not Quite So) Plain Pound Cake
*Classic or Chocolate Sponge Cake
Marble Cake

Chocolate Sour Cream Topping

Yield: 2¾ cups

The perfect match for chocolate cake, this topping drapes each slice like a soft blanket.

2 ounces unsweetened chocolate
¼ cup (½ stick) unsalted butter
1 cup sour cream
2 cups confectioners' sugar
1 teaspoon vanilla extract

1. Cut chocolate and butter into small pieces. Combine in a glass measuring cup or small bowl. Microwave on high power until the chocolate is almost melted, 1 to 1½ minutes. Remove from microwave oven and stir until completely melted. Or melt chocolate with butter in a double boiler over barely simmering water (see Index, "How to Melt Chocolate").

2. Transfer melted chocolate mixture to the bowl of a mixer. Beat in mixer on medium-low speed for 1 to 2 minutes to cool slightly. Add sour cream and, when blended, add sugar, ½ cup at a time, blending after each addition. Add vanilla and mix until smooth. Refrigerate until cooled.

3. Spread over top of cooled cake before slicing, or spoon onto cake slices before serving.

Note: This topping can be made ahead, covered, and refrigerated for up to 3 days.

CAKES SUGGESTED FOR THIS TOPPING

★Chocolate Layer Cake
★(Not Quite So) Plain Pound Cake
★Banana Bundt Cake

Cinnamon Cream Topping

Yield: 3 cups

Soft, glossy, and seductive. Try this with just about any cake.

1 package (8 ounces) cream cheese, at room temperature
1 cup sour cream
1 teaspoon ground cinnamon
1½ cups confectioners' sugar

1. Combine cream cheese and sour cream in mixer. Beat on medium speed until smooth.

2. Reduce mixer speed to low, add cinnamon, and begin adding sugar, ½ cup at a time. Scrape down ingredients with rubber spatula as necessary. Mix until smoothly blended.

3. Spread over top of cooled cake before slicing, or spoon onto cake slices before serving.

Note: This topping can be made ahead, covered, and refrigerated for up to 3 days.

Garnish tip: Lightly sprinkle extra cinnamon onto topping before serving.

CAKES SUGGESTED FOR THIS TOPPING

*Applesauce or Banana Bundt Cake
*(Not Quite So) Plain or Praline Pound Cake
*Cheesecake or Strawberry or Mocha Cheesecake
*Chocolate Layer Cake
Gingerbread
Spice Cake

Orange Cream-Cheese Topping

Yield: 2 cups

Ivory colored with a soft, pudding-like texture, this topping adds a touch of luxury.

1 cup orange juice
½ cup granulated sugar
1 tablespoon cornstarch
1 package (8 ounces) cream cheese, at room temperature

1. Combine orange juice, sugar, and cornstarch in a small saucepan. Whisk to blend ingredients. Turn on heat to medium and bring mixture to a boil, stirring occasionally. Boil 1 minute and remove from heat. Cool to room temperature. (You can speed the cooling by transferring mixture to a bowl and chilling it in the refrigerator. If it becomes colder than room temperature, that's fine.)

2. Beat the cream cheese in mixer on medium speed until soft. Add the cooled orange mixture. Increase mixer speed to medium high and beat until ingredients are smoothly blended, about 1 minute. Spoon onto cake slices before serving.

Note: This topping can be made ahead, covered, and refrigerated for up to 3 days.

CAKES SUGGESTED FOR THIS TOPPING

*Applesauce or Banana Bundt Cake
*(Not Quite So) Plain or Lemon Pound Cake
Pineapple Upside-Down Cake
Carrot Cake
Spice Cake

Blueberries and Cream Topping

Yield: 2 cups

If you have enough blueberries, you might want to double the recipe. This topping is so good you'll be serving it alone after the cake is gone.

1 cup blueberries, fresh or frozen
½ teaspoon grated lemon rind (1 lemon)
2 tablespoons freshly squeezed lemon juice
¼ cup granulated sugar
1½ teaspoons cornstarch
½ cup whipping cream

1. Combine blueberries, lemon rind and juice, sugar, and cornstarch in a nonaluminum saucepan. Turn heat to medium and bring the mixture to a boil, stirring occasionally. Boil 1 minute and remove from heat. Pour into a bowl and cool. (If convenient, make ahead, cover, and refrigerate. Proceed when ready.)
2. Whip cream in mixer on medium speed until soft peaks form. Fold the cooled blueberry mixture into the cream until blended. Spread over top of cooled cake before slicing, or spoon onto cake slices before serving.

Note: This topping can be made ahead, covered, and refrigerated for up to 1 day before using.

CAKES SUGGESTED FOR THIS TOPPING

*Cheesecake
*(Not Quite So) Plain or Lemon Pound Cake
*Basic Butter Cake (White or Yellow)
Angel Food Cake

Pineapple-Orange Topping

Yield: 1⅔ cups

A cool and refreshing treat. Use this when you want a light topping.

1 can (8 ounces) crushed pineapple, drained
½ cup orange marmalade
½ cup orange juice
1 tablespoon cornstarch

1. Combine drained pineapple and marmalade in a small saucepan.
2. Stir orange juice and cornstarch together to blend. Add to the pineapple mixture in saucepan. Stir to mix.
3. Turn on heat to medium low and stir while bringing mixture to a boil. Boil 30 seconds, and then remove from heat.
4. Pour into a bowl and let cool completely before using. Spread over top of cooled cake before slicing, or spoon onto cake slices before serving.

Note: This topping can be made ahead, covered, and refrigerated for up to 5 days.

Garnish tip: Toasted coconut sprinkled on top adds an interesting crunch (see Index).

CAKES SUGGESTED FOR THIS TOPPING

*Cheesecake
*Basic Butter Cake (White or Yellow)
*Banana Bundt Cake
*(Not Quite So) Plain Pound Cake
Carrot Cake
Spice Cake

Sweet-Cherry Topping

Yield: 1¾ cups

Rich, sweet, and just a bit tart, canned cherries take on an elegant air with the help of just a few simple additional ingredients.

1 can (16 ounces) dark sweet cherries in syrup
(½ cup syrup reserved)
1 tablespoon cornstarch
2 tablespoons honey
1½ teaspoons lemon juice
¼ teaspoon ground cinnamon

1. Drain canned cherries over a bowl and reserve ½ cup of the syrup. Set cherries aside. Combine cornstarch with the reserved syrup in a saucepan and stir to mix.

2. Add honey, lemon juice, and cinnamon to syrup. Turn on heat to medium low and stir while bringing to a boil. Add the cherries, stir, and bring back to a boil. Boil 30 seconds and remove from heat.

3. Pour into a bowl and let cool completely. Spread over top of cooled cake before slicing, or spoon onto cake slices before serving.

Note: This topping can be made ahead, covered, and refrigerated for up to 5 days.

CAKES SUGGESTED FOR THIS TOPPING

*Cheesecake
*Chocolate Layer Cake
*Basic Butter Cake (White or Yellow)
*(Not Quite So) Plain Pound Cake

11
Sauces

Sauces and cakes are made for each other. A creamy sauce, pooled under or poured over a slice of cake, provides both a textural contrast and an exciting taste variation. Sauces are wonderful for another reason as well. They can turn a slightly flawed cake into an applause-winning success because they mask mistakes. Cake too dry? Sauce it! Slice crumbled? Sauce it! Flavor too bland? A sauce will add the needed flavor boost.

You will find that making sauces for cakes is really quite easy. A few quick steps, very little mess, and it's done. Most of the sauces in this chapter can be made ahead, keep well, and make terrific gifts.

Vanilla Sauce

Yield: 1½ cups

This is the quintessential sauce for any cake. Since vanilla leads all other ice cream flavors in popularity, you know you have a winner here.

1 cup whole milk
2 large eggs
3 tablespoons granulated sugar
1 teaspoon vanilla extract

1. Place milk in a small saucepan. Warm over low heat until hot but not quite simmering.

2. Meanwhile, stir eggs and sugar together in a bowl with a whisk. Pour the hot milk into the egg mixture while stirring. Return this mixture to the saucepan over low heat. Using a wooden spoon, continue to stir until sauce just barely thickens. Do not allow it to simmer. This should take no more than 5 minutes. (The sauce will leave a thin coating on the back side of your stirring spoon when it is ready to be removed from the heat.) Immediately pour into a bowl to prevent the eggs from curdling the sauce.

3. Stir in vanilla. Cover the surface with waxed paper to prevent a skin from forming and refrigerate until chilled. Cover with plastic wrap when chilled.

4. The sauce will keep in the refrigerator for up to 1 week. Remove from refrigerator 30 minutes before serving.

CAKES SUGGESTED FOR THIS SAUCE

*Chocolate Layer Cake
*Classic or Chocolate Sponge Cake
*Applesauce or Banana Bundt Cake
*(Not Quite So) Plain, Lemon, or Praline Pound Cake
Spice Cake

Strawberry Sauce

༄

Yield: 2½ cups

When strawberries are in season, use ripe, fresh berries for this spritely sauce. Adjust the amount of sugar to suit your taste.

2 cups fresh strawberries, or *1 package (16 ounces) frozen unsweetened strawberries, thawed*
⅓ cup orange juice
2 tablespoons granulated sugar

1. Puree strawberries with orange juice and sugar in an electric blender until smooth.
2. The sauce will keep in the refrigerator for up to 1 week. Remove from refrigerator 30 minutes before serving.

CAKES SUGGESTED FOR THIS SAUCE

*Banana Bundt Cake
*Chocolate Layer Cake
*Classic or Chocolate Sponge Cake
*Cheesecake, Strawberry or Mocha Cheesecake
Angel Food Cake

Fresh Pear Sauce

Yield: 2 cups

This sauce has a delightfully fresh, sweet, pear flavor when ripe pears (softened and aromatic) are used. Expect the sauce color to darken to a light caramel. Pear brandy is really a plus in this recipe, as even a small amount intensifies the natural pear flavor. French, Swiss, and American brands are available in most wine and spirits stores.

¼ cup granulated sugar
¼ cup water
1 pound ripe pears
1½ teaspoons freshly squeezed lemon juice
1 tablespoon pear brandy

1. Combine sugar and water in a small saucepan. Bring to a boil over medium heat while stirring to melt the sugar. Boil 3 minutes and remove from heat. Set aside.
2. Peel, core, and seed pears. Cut each into 8 pieces. Puree with the sugar syrup, lemon juice, and pear brandy in an electric blender. (Add more sugar to taste.)
3. The sauce will keep in the refrigerator for up to 3 days. Remove from refrigerator 30 minutes before serving.

CAKES SUGGESTED FOR THIS SAUCE

*(Not Quite So) Plain, Lemon, or Praline Pound Cake
*Cheesecake
*Classic or Chocolate Sponge Cake
Spice Cake

Raspberry Crème Fraîche

Yield: 2½ cups

A beautiful lavender-colored sauce with a deluxe fruit flavor. Spoon softly onto cake slices, or refrigerate to firm it up and spread as a topping on your cake.

1 cup raspberry jam
¼ cup brandy
2 cups crème fraîche (See Note for substitution)

1. Combine jam and brandy in a small saucepan. Bring to a boil over medium heat, stirring occasionally. Boil 3 minutes and remove from heat. Pour into a bowl and cool. (You can make this ahead, cover, and set aside at room temperature for up to 3 days. Proceed with the final step when convenient.)

2. Stir cooled raspberry mixture into crème fraîche until smoothly blended. Use immediately or cover and refrigerate for up to 1 week before using. Remove from refrigerator 30 minutes before serving.

Note: Crème fraîche is sold in the dairy section of some supermarkets. If unavailable, use this creamy substitute: whip ½ cup whipping cream to soft peaks. Stir it into 1 cup sour cream.

CAKES SUGGESTED FOR THIS SAUCE

*Chocolate Layer Cake
*Cheesecake or Strawberry Cheesecake
*(Not Quite So) Plain or Lemon Pound Cake
*Banana Bundt Cake

Peach Yogurt Sauce

Yield: 2¾ cups

You'll want to bring out the soup spoons when you serve this delicious, light, fruity sauce. In addition to serving it with cake, try it at breakfast with hot oatmeal or cold muesli (mixed whole-grain cereal).

*1 package (16 ounces) frozen unsweetened sliced peaches,
  thawed
1 cup vanilla flavored yogurt
3 tablespoons packed light brown sugar*

1. Puree peaches with yogurt and sugar in an electric blender until smooth.
2. The sauce will keep in the refrigerator for up to 1 week. Remove from refrigerator 30 minutes before serving.

CAKES SUGGESTED FOR THIS SAUCE

*(Not Quite So) Plain or Lemon Pound Cake
*Banana Bundt Cake
Spice Cake
Angel Food Cake

Lemon Sauce

Yield: 2 cups

Sweet and tart all at once, this sauce is reasonably assertive and leaves you wanting more. It's at its best when used on subtly flavored cakes such as pound cake.

1 cup granulated sugar
⅔ cup freshly squeezed lemon juice (2 large lemons)
2 large eggs
1½ tablespoons arrowroot or cornstarch
½ cup (1 stick) unsalted butter, cut into tablespoon-size
  pieces

1. Combine sugar, lemon juice, eggs, and arrowroot in a nonaluminum saucepan. Stir to blend ingredients. Turn heat to low and cook, stirring constantly, until thickened (do not boil or sauce will curdle).

2. Remove from heat and immediately stir in the butter, 1 tablespoon at a time, as each melts. Pour into a bowl and cool.

3. The sauce will keep in the refrigerator for up to 1 week. Remove from refrigerator 30 minutes before serving.

CAKES SUGGESTED FOR THIS SAUCE

*(Not Quite So) Plain or Lemon Pound Cake
*Basic Butter Cake (White or Yellow)
*Banana Bundt Cake
*Cheesecake
Gingerbread

Dark Butterscotch Sauce

Yield: 1½ cups

Any apple or banana cake will be improved with the addition of this decadently indulgent sauce. Serve this sauce also if ice cream or brownies make an appearance for dessert.

1 cup packed dark brown sugar
½ cup whipping cream
¼ cup (½ stick) unsalted butter
¼ cup light corn syrup

1. Combine sugar, cream, butter, and syrup in a saucepan. Bring to a boil while stirring over medium heat. Boil 5 minutes and remove from heat.
2. Pour into a bowl and cool to warm before serving.
3. The sauce will keep in the refrigerator for up to 2 weeks. Reheat until pourable before serving. (Sauce can be reheated in a microwave oven.)

Cakes Suggested for This Sauce

*Applesauce or Banana Bundt Cake
*(Not Quite So) Plain or Praline Pound Cake
*Cheesecake, Strawberry or Mocha Cheesecake
Spice Cake
Pecan or Walnut Cake

Chocolate Rum Sauce

Yield: 1⅓ cups

Dark, dense, rich chocolate is enhanced with the discreet addition of rum. A jar of this sauce would make a welcome gift for chocolate-loving friends. Be sure to warm the thickened sauce before pouring over cake slices.

2 ounces unsweetened chocolate
¼ cup (½ stick) unsalted butter
½ cup packed light brown sugar
½ cup whipping cream
1½ tablespoons rum, preferably dark

1. Cut chocolate and butter into small pieces and combine with sugar and cream in a saucepan. Set over low heat and stir just until all the ingredients are melted and blended. Remove from heat.

2. Stir in rum and pour into a bowl to cool and thicken. Allow at least 2 hours at room temperature.

3. The sauce will keep in the refrigerator for up to 2 weeks. Warm just until pourable before serving. (Sauce can be rewarmed in a microwave oven.)

CAKES SUGGESTED FOR THIS SAUCE

*Chocolate Layer Cake
*(Not Quite So) Plain or Praline Pound Cake
*Banana Bundt Cake
*Basic Butter Cake (White or Yellow)

Café Mocha Sauce

Yield: 1½ cups

This sauce has two wonderful attributes—a rich coffee flavor and a smooth, velvet consistency. Once you've tried it, you'll mark this recipe for a repeat performance.

1 cup whipping cream
½ cup granulated sugar
2 tablespoons instant espresso coffee granules
¼ cup coffee liqueur
2 teaspoons cornstarch
2 ounces (¼ cup) semisweet chocolate chips

1. Combine cream, sugar, and espresso in a small saucepan.

2. Combine liqueur and cornstarch in a small bowl and stir to blend. Set near stove top.

3. Bring cream mixture to a boil while stirring over medium-low heat. Add the cornstarch mixture, stir, and bring back to a boil. Boil for 30 seconds and remove from heat.

4. Immediately stir in chocolate chips until completely melted. Pour into a bowl and cool. Serve this sauce warm, at room temperature, or chilled.

5. The sauce will keep in the refrigerator for up to 1 week. Remove from refrigerator 30 minutes before serving.

CAKES SUGGESTED FOR THIS SAUCE

★Chocolate Layer Cake
★(Not Quite So) Plain Pound Cake
★Banana Bundt Cake

Hazelnut Hard Sauce

Yield: 1⅔ cups

You will want to spoon this atop warm cake slices to experience the full nutty flavor of a barely melting, butter-rich sauce. For a spectacular holiday dessert, serve this sauce with a warm steamed pudding.

½ cup (1 stick) unsalted butter, at room temperature
½ cup (2 ounces) finely ground hazelnuts
1 cup confectioners' sugar
¼ cup Frangelico (hazelnut liqueur)

1. Cream butter with hazelnuts in a mixer on medium speed until smoothly blended.
2. Add sugar and mix, scraping down sides of bowl as necessary. Slowly pour in liqueur, blending until smooth.
3. Cover and set aside at room temperature for up to 2 days before using. To serve, spoon sauce onto warm cake slices.
4. Sauce can be made ahead and refrigerated for up to 2 weeks. Return to room temperature before using.

CAKES SUGGESTED FOR THIS SAUCE

*Applesauce or Banana Bundt Cake
*(Not Quite So) Plain or Lemon Pound Cake
Carrot Cake
Spice Cake

12
Garnishes

There are times when after frosting, icing, or glazing a cake, you still want to further dress it up. Garnishing a cake offers you an opportunity to be creative and inventive—and to have fun. Not only can a garnish hide minor flaws but it can also provide the extra glitter that will cause family and guests to take notice. The ten recipes in this chapter are for garnishes that are best made prior to the hour of need, although none are difficult or require special skills. Try them, and then create some of your own. You even can improvise with items already in your pantry.

Here are some suggestions for quickly made garnishes:

- Press sliced almonds, chopped nuts, or crushed candy onto frosted cake sides with the palm of your hand, or sprinkle them atop your cake immediately after frosting it.

- Sprinkle cake top with ground cinnamon, nutmeg, or allspice. Apply the spice by rubbing it between your forefinger and thumb to ensure a light dusting.

- Sprinkle cake with confectioners' sugar or cocoa powder by spooning either one into a small fine-mesh sieve. Tap the side of the sieve gently with the palm of your hand to release a controlled flow over cake top. For a patterned effect, place a lacey doily atop the (unfrosted) cake and then sprinkle heavily with sugar or cocoa. Carefully remove and discard doily. A paper stencil can be used this way as well.

- Decorate with chocolate. Melt a small number of semisweet chocolate pieces by placing them in a small plastic bag. Set closed bag in a shallow bowl of hot water. When chocolate has melted, snip the tip off the end of one corner of the bag and drizzle the chocolate atop the cake in a circular or zigzag pattern (Lemon Icing [see Index] can be pressed through a bag in the same manner.)

- Comb cake sides with a fork. After frosting, hold pointed tines of fork perpendicular against the side of the cake. If the cake is on a turntable, rotate it to create light, even, combing strokes (horizontal ribbing). Without a turntable, rotate the cake plate in quarter turns. Either way, repeat until frosted sides are completely combed. A cake top can be done the same way. You can purchase a baker's comb in cookware stores.

- Decorate with toasted nuts. Spread whole almonds, pecan halves, or walnut halves on a sheet pan in a single layer. Bake in the middle of a 375°F oven until golden brown and crisp, about 10 minutes. Cool before using. Place on frosted cake sides or top.

Here is a list of supermarket items that can be invaluable in creating impromptu cake garnishes:

Candy: use crushed, chopped, or whole if very small
Cookies: use crushed, or place whole thin wafer cookies on cake rim
Banana chips and candied nuts: use chopped or whole
Colored chocolate disks and colored chocolate mints
Colored sprinkles and chocolate sprinkles
Red cinnamon candies and colored beads
Candied violets
Dried mixed fruit: use diced or chopped
Chocolate twigs
Chocolate coffee beans

In this chapter, all of the recipes for frostings, fillings, icings, glazes, and toppings suggested for use on cakes can be found in this book.

Macadamia Nut Brittle

Yield: approximately 2 cups

Use this brittle in broken pieces atop a cake, or chop it up and press it onto frosted cake sides. It is delicious on ice cream as well.

1 tablespoon vegetable oil
1 jar (3½ ounces) macadamia nuts
2 tablespoons unsalted butter
¼ teaspoon baking soda
1 cup granulated sugar
⅓ cup light corn syrup
3 tablespoons water

1. Grease a metal spatula and the bottom of a 13″ × 9″ sheet pan with the vegetable oil, using a paper towel. Set near stove top.

2. Coarsely chop the nuts, cut butter into chunks, and measure out baking soda. Set near stove top.

3. Combine sugar, corn syrup, and water in a medium saucepan and bring to a boil over medium heat. Boil until mixture turns an even tan color, about 10 minutes. Remove from heat and immediately stir in nuts, butter, and soda. Mix just until foam starts to subside, and then pour onto greased sheet pan. Quickly spread as thinly as possible with the greased spatula. (Brittle will begin to set soon after being removed from heat.) Set aside to cool and harden, at least 30 minutes.

4. Crack the brittle into pieces. Store in airtight container at room temperature for up to 2 months.

CAKES AND FROSTINGS SUGGESTED FOR THIS GARNISH

*Cheesecake (without topping)
*Chocolate Layer Cake with Southern Meringue Fluff Frosting
Carrot Cake with Cream Cheese Frosting with Orange Peel
    or Coconut Cream Frosting
Spice Cake with White-Chocolate Dream Frosting

Praline

Yield: 1 cup

This crushed-nut and sugar garnish can be used in cake batters as well as sprinkled atop cake or pressed onto cake sides. When using it in cake batters, reduce sugar slightly (see Index, "Praline Pound Cake").

1 tablespoon vegetable oil
½ cup (2 ounces) sliced almonds
½ cup granulated sugar
1 tablespoon light corn syrup

1. Grease the bottom of a 13″ × 9″ sheet pan with the vegetable oil, using a paper towel. Spread almonds out on pan center, overlapping without forming a pile. Set aside.

2. Combine sugar and syrup in a small skillet. Bring to a boil over medium heat, swirling the pan slightly to evenly distribute sugar as it melts. Let mixture boil until it turns a medium-brown color. Immediately remove it from heat and pour over the almonds to cover evenly. Set aside to cool and harden, at least 30 minutes.

3. Crush hardened mixture in a grinder or food processor or by hand. To crush by hand: cover with a clean towel and crush with a rolling pin. May be stored in airtight container at room temperature for up to 2 months.

CAKES AND FROSTINGS SUGGESTED FOR THIS GARNISH

*Praline Pound Cake
*Cheesecake
*Basic Butter Cake (White) with Velvety Chocolate Frosting
*Sponge Cake Roll with Praline Buttercream Frosting

Sugar-and-Spice Nut Crunch

Yield: 1⅓ cups

Toasted nuts covered in sugar and cinnamon are crunchy and sweet. This garnish, similar to streusel, also can be sprinkled atop coffee cake.

2 tablespoons unsalted butter
1 cup (4 ounces) coarsely chopped nuts (walnuts, pecans, almonds, or hazelnuts)
⅓ cup granulated sugar
½ teaspoon ground cinnamon

1. Heat oven to 300°F. Melt butter in a small saucepan over low heat. Add nuts and stir to coat evenly with the butter.
2. Remove from heat and stir in sugar and cinnamon. Mix thoroughly.
3. Spread mixture on a sheet pan and bake in oven until nuts are toasted, about 30 minutes.
4. Cool and store in airtight container at room temperature for up to 2 weeks. Refrigerate for up to 2 months.

CAKES AND FROSTINGS SUGGESTED FOR THIS GARNISH

*Applesauce or Banana Bundt Cake with Rum-Butter or Banana Icing
*(Not Quite So) Plain Pound Cake with Maple Syrup or Coffee Liqueur Glaze
*Cheesecake with Tropical Fruit Glaze
*Basic Butter Cake (Yellow) with Cranberry Cream Cheese Frosting

Toasted Coconut

Yield: 1½ cups

Sweetened flaked coconut can easily burn in the oven, so your strict attention is necessary for the few minutes it takes to prepare this garnish. The result is a pretty mix of light, medium, and dark toasted flakes.

1½ cups sweetened flaked coconut

1. Heat oven to 350°F. Spread coconut in an even layer on a small baking pan.

2. Bake 5 minutes. Remove coconut from oven and stir. Return it to oven for 5 more minutes (but no more than 5). Immediately remove it from oven and transfer to a bowl. Stir again and set aside to cool.

3. May be stored in airtight container at room temperature for up to 2 months.

CAKES AND FROSTINGS SUGGESTED FOR THIS GARNISH

*Chocolate Layer Cake with White-Chocolate Dream Frosting
*Basic Butter Cake (White) with Better-Than-Fudge Frosting
 Carrot Cake with Coconut Cream Frosting
 Spice Cake with Apricot Cheese Frosting

White-Chocolate Fruit Pieces

Yield: 1 cup

Use small dried fruit, such as raisins, sweet dried cherries, and dried cranberries for this garnish. Arrange in bull's-eye rings atop cake. You should keep some extra pieces on hand for a tasty snack.

3 ounces (1 bar) white chocolate made with cocoa butter
½ cup dried fruit (small or cut into pieces)

1. Cut white chocolate into small pieces. Place in a glass bowl and microwave on high power until almost melted, about 1½ minutes. Remove from microwave oven and stir until completely melted. Or place in a double boiler over barely simmering water and remove from heat before completely melted. Stir until melted.

2. Stir fruit into the melted white chocolate, evenly coating all the fruit. Spread fruit out on waxed paper or aluminum foil in a single layer to cool and harden. Break apart into individual pieces before using.

3. May be stored in airtight container at room temperature for up to 2 months.

CAKES AND FROSTINGS SUGGESTED FOR THIS GARNISH

*Cheesecake with Tropical Fruit Glaze
*Basic Butter Cake (White) with Velvety Chocolate Frosting
Carrot Cake with Coconut Cream Frosting
Spice Cake with Apricot Cheese Frosting

Glazed Citrus Peel

Yield: enough for 1 cake

Lemon, lime, or orange peel is cooked in a simple sugar syrup to give it a sweet, clear glaze. This garnish adds a tart, crisp zing to frosted cakes.

1 lemon, lime, or orange
¼ cup granulated sugar
¼ cup water

1. Using a citrus peeler (see Index), or a vegetable peeler, remove peel in vertical strips from the fruit. Wide strips, from a vegetable peeler, must be cut into very thin strips with a knife. Refrigerate the skinless fruit for another use.

2. Combine sugar and water in a small saucepan. Bring to a boil over medium heat. Boil 2 minutes.

3. Add citrus peel strips, completely covering them with syrup. Boil 2 minutes and then remove from heat. With tongs, remove strips from hot syrup and place them on a sheet of waxed paper or aluminum foil, spreading them out so they don't overlap. (Strips will twist and curl as you place them on the paper.) Set aside to cool and dry. Discard syrup.

4. May be stored in airtight container in a cool place for up to 5 days.

CAKES AND FROSTINGS SUGGESTED FOR THIS GARNISH

*(Not Quite So) Plain Pound Cake with Lemon Icing

*Applesauce or Banana Bundt Cake with Tropical Fruit Glaze

*Classic Sponge Cake with Lemon Cream or Orange
    Buttercream Frosting

Easy Glazed Strawberries

Yield: enough for 1 cake

Perfect for Cheesecake (see Index). A garnish of glistening berries atop each creamy slice has plenty of eye appeal.

2 pints fresh strawberries
⅓ cup currant jelly

1. Wash and hull berries, discarding any that are bruised or very soft. Dry in paper toweling. Position whole berries, hulled-side down, atop cake; or slice berries and arrange in overlapping concentric circles atop cake.
2. Place jelly in a small glass bowl and microwave on high power to melt, about 50 seconds. Or melt jelly in a small saucepan over low heat until warm.
3. Brush whole or sliced berries with warm jelly to coat evenly.

CAKES AND FROSTINGS SUGGESTED FOR THIS GARNISH

*Cheesecake or Strawberry Cheesecake
*Classic or Chocolate Sponge Cake with Raspberry
  Buttercream Frosting
*Classic Sponge Cake with Whipped Cream Filling

Sugared Fruit, Mint Leaves, and Flower Petals

Sugar-coated edible garniture creates a stunning presentation for a frosted cake or a serving plate. Whatever produce you use should be fresh and in peak condition; flowers should be freshly opened. Select any of the following: green or red seedless grapes (individual or in small clusters), strawberries with green tops, raspberries, blueberries, young rose petals, or violets. Snip off large individual mint leaves and the cluster of tiny leaves at each sprig tip, discarding stem.

1. If you are using fruit, wash and thoroughly dry it.
2. Beat an egg white in a small bowl with a fork until bubbly, but not frothy.
3. Arrange a layer of granulated sugar on a sheet of waxed paper.
4. Using a fine brush, paint the fruit, leaves, or petals with the egg white, covering them completely. Place them on the sugar-lined paper. Immediately, using a fine-mesh sieve, sift more granulated sugar on top of the fruit, leaves, or petals. Cover thickly and evenly with sugar, and then scrape off any clumps.
5. Transfer sugared pieces to a clean sheet of waxed paper, shaking off excess sugar, and set aside to dry. Use within 24 hours.

COMPLEMENTS FOR THESE GARNISHES

*Raspberry Buttercream Frosting for sugared raspberries
    or rose petals
*Lemon Cream Frosting or *Whipped Mint Cream
  Topping for sugared mint leaves
*Cinnamon Cream Topping for sugared strawberries

Chocolate Shapes and Curls

Shapes and curls made of chocolate add a dramatic finishing touch, particularly to cakes frosted with chocolate. Although these garnishes are not difficult to make, working with chocolate can be intimidating for the uninitiated. Read "How to Melt Chocolate" (see Index) before beginning.

To make chocolate shapes:

1. Cut 4 ounces of semisweet chocolate into small pieces. Place in a glass bowl and microwave on high power until almost melted, about 1½ minutes. Remove and stir until completely melted and smooth. Or melt chocolate in a double boiler over barely simmering water until almost melted. Stir until completely melted and smooth.

2. Pour onto center of a cookie sheet. Spread with a thin metal spatula in even back and forth strokes into a 10-inch square. Refrigerate until set, about 15 minutes. Remove from refrigerator and let soften just slightly. (Shapes will crack if chocolate is too hard.) Allow about 5 minutes.

3. Press small cookie cutters or canapé cutters into chocolate to make as many shapes as desired. Lift shapes up with a metal spatula and transfer them to a waxed paper-lined plate, touching them as little as possible. Refrigerate until ready to use. Any remaining chocolate can be scraped up and stored in an airtight container for another use.

To make chocolate curls:

1. Unwrap a bar of milk chocolate (or white chocolate) and cut in half. For a few seconds, hold one of the halves between the palms of your hands and press to soften just slightly.

2. Place the chocolate piece, smooth-side up, on a countertop or hold it in a paper towel in one hand. Using a vegetable peeler, begin at the outside edge and scrape into curls. If chocolate cracks into pieces instead of curls, rewarm it in your hands and try again. Lift curls up with a metal spatula and transfer them to a waxed paper-lined plate, without further handling. Refrigerate until ready to use.

Chocolate-Coated Fruit and Chocolate Leaves

Big red strawberries with fresh green tops are the best fresh fruit for dipping in chocolate. You can dip either the tips, half the berry, or the whole berry up to the green. Glazed apricots half coated in chocolate also look great. Buy green leaves from a florist, selecting those with texture and ribbing. (Be sure you purchase nonpoisonous leaves!) Read "How to Melt Chocolate" (see Index) before beginning.

To coat fruit and leaves:

1. You will need between 4 and 8 ounces of semisweet chocolate, depending on the number you want to coat. Cut chocolate into small pieces and place in a glass bowl. Microwave on high power until almost melted, 1½ to 2 minutes. Remove from microwave oven and stir until completely melted. Or melt chocolate in a double boiler over barely simmering water. Stir until it is smooth and remove from heat.

2. For fruit: Hold each strawberry by the green top and dip it into the melted chocolate, covering as desired. Dip each glazed apricot until half covered. Hold the fruit above the chocolate after dipping to allow excess to drip off. Set dipped fruit on a waxed paper-lined tray or plate. Refrigerate until ready to use.

3. For leaves: Hold each leaf by the stem. Using a fine brush, paint the underside (textured side) of the leaf with the melted chocolate in a smooth even layer—neither too thick nor too thin. Place each leaf, painted-side up, on a waxed paper-lined tray or plate. Refrigerate until hardened and set. Peel off the green leaf, pulling by the stem end, and touching the chocolate as little as possible. Return the chocolate leaves to the refrigerator until ready to use. Any remaining chocolate can be stored in an airtight container for another use.

Index